Literature
Study Circles
in a Multicultural
Classroom

Literature Study Circles in a Multicultural Classroom

Katharine Davies Samway
Gail Whang

Stenhouse Publishers
Portland, Maine

Stenhouse Publishers

Library of Congress Cataloging-in-Publication Data

Samway, Katharine Davies.
    Literature study circles in a multicultural classroom /
Katharine Davies Samway, Gail Whang.
        p.   cm.
    Includes bibliographical references.
    ISBN 1-57110-018-0 (alk. paper)
    1. Literature—Study and teaching (Elementary)—
United States.   2. Minorities—Education (Elementary)—
United States.   3. Group reading—United States.
4. Group work in education—United States.
I. Whang, Gail.   II. Title.
LB1576S248   1995
372.64—dc20   95-33304
                                                          CIP

Cover and interior design by Joyce C. Weston

Cover photograph by Katharine Davies Samway

Typeset by Achorn Graphics

Manufactured in the United States of America
on acid-free paper
06 05 04 03 02 01 9 8 7 6 5 4

*To our students, from whom we learned
the importance of listening to and including
children's voices in classroom events*

Contents

Acknowledgments

Kathy Maloney and Barbara Schmidt are friends and colleagues from whom we have learned a great deal. Several years ago, they invited Katharine into their classrooms at Sequoia Elementary School in Oakland, California, to help them implement LSCs. Neither of us could have ever understood the potential impact of LSCs on both children and adults if we had not had the opportunity to work so closely with such talented and thoughtful teachers—and to work just as closely with their equally talented students. We have also seen the power of LSCs through the eyes of our children, when they were students in Kathy's and Barbara's classrooms.

We are grateful to Cindy Pease-Alvarez, who introduced us to Fair Oaks School, where we first encountered LSCs. Cindy also worked closely with Katharine in implementing LSCs with teachers in the 1987–88 school year. It was Cindy who gently pointed out the importance of wait time and silence in discussions.

Kathy Booker is a wonderful colleague who taught next door to Gail. She offers the kind of collegiality that makes it possible to take on new challenges. We spent many hours during recess and at lunchtime sharing our excitement about LSCs, talking about the impact of LSCs on students, and exploring problems we encountered. We have learned so much from Kathy's reflective and thorough approach to teaching.

Arlene Graham was a principal who always encouraged teachers to be informed innovators. She always had time for us to brainstorm ideas, questions, and approaches. As a woman of action who is a good listener, respectful of teachers, and comfortable working with teachers who take initiative, she is an inspiration to us.

Susan Sperber has been a good friend throughout the whole process of learning about, implementing, and writing about LSCs. We have learned so much from her about the importance of knowing students in the most complete way possible. The care and warmth that she shows for her students has had a profound impact on us.

Sonja Ebel job-shared with Gail for two years, and those two years were filled with stimulating conversation and new ideas that inspired Gail to experiment more than ever before. Sonja was always quick to expand and improve on existing practices. Her passionate resourcefulness enabled us to provide more multicultural literature for the students.

Sonny Kim was a student teacher who immediately became a colleague. His thoughtfulness and desire to learn helped stimulate our thinking. It is always a pleasure to work with colleagues who take the kind of initiative that Sonny does. On many occasions, he would use the computer to turn roughly-sketched ideas into well-thought-through procedures that were very helpful to students and other teachers, as well as to us.

Many of the intermediate grade teachers at Hawthorne School would meet on a regular basis to learn about LSCs through engaging in book discussions. These meetings were stimulating and helped us to better understand and implement LSCs in our classrooms. We are particularly grateful for the support that Kathy Booker, Mike Bowen, Mike Cooper, Sonia Diermayer, Doug Dohrer, Sonja Ebel, Robert Harhay, Lisa Hiltbrand, Jesse Inclan, Julie Landswerk, Rosalie Le Count, Unkyung Park, Sara Steck, and Vera Watson gave us. Their candor and openness to learning were inspirational and helped deepen our understanding.

Although LSCs can be implemented without additional adult support in the classroom, we have been blessed with the help of several talented instructional aides. We are indebted to Hilda Menjivar, Somsy Phonexaysitthidet, Diana KountheaSo, Rosie Rodriguez, and Nitayane Youmagul. They were particularly helpful when clarifying cross-cultural and language issues.

From time to time we were fortunate to have volunteers working in the classroom. Marci Chentow was particularly skillful at leading LSCs, even before she fully understood what was involved. She had a wonderful ability to lead discussions in which students shared in profound ways. Ginger Smith interacted with struggling students with remarkable compassion and understanding—she helped several children begin to see themselves as readers.

We owe a great debt to the teachers at Fair Oaks School in Redwood City, California, where we first saw teachers and children engaged in LSCs. The excitement that was generated in those classrooms was thrilling and compelled us to become much more knowledgeable about the theory underpinning LSCs, as well as their actual practice. We learned so much from observing and talking with these skilled teachers. We are particularly grateful to Leslie Mangiola, Gloria Norton, and Pat Yencho for welcoming us into their school and classrooms and for sharing their insights so freely.

Although we never had the opportunity to visit Karen Smith's class in Arizona, we owe her a huge debt, as it was Karen and Carole Edelsky who had such a profound impact on the Fair Oaks teachers introducing their students to LSCs. We continue to learn from them when reading their articles and hearing them speak at conferences.

When we began to record LSCs, we knew that we had a huge task ahead of us in transcribing the tapes. Although we did a lot of the transcribing ourselves, we were helped a great deal by Melinda Nettles, Raiida Thompson, and Susana Mangney, who not only transcribed the tapes, but gave us useful feedback on what they heard.

Several practicing and preservice teachers have read chapters of this book, including Melinda Nettles and Carolyn Downey. We found their comments and insights to be very helpful.

We have received small grants that assisted us in significant ways in implementing LSCs and writing this book. The Marcus A. Foster Educational Institute awarded Gail two grants for the purchasing of books for LSCs. San José State University Research Foundation provided funds for a research assistant, which proved invaluable.

Philippa Stratton, Stenhouse editor, first suggested this book several years ago. It has been a wonderful undertaking to work so closely with her. She brings tremendous knowledge about children's literacy development and a keen eye for writing clearly and evocatively, and we are very grateful for all the time she spent with us. We are also very grateful for the personable, meticulous, and considerate way in which Martha Drury and Tom Seavey at Stenhouse, and Donna Bouvier, the copyeditor, worked with us to bring the book into publication.

For over twenty-five years Gail has shared her ideas, thoughts, and hopes with her cousin, Brenda Paik Sunoo. At major junctures in Gail's life, Brenda has been present with support and astute advice.

Writing can be an all-consuming task, particularly when one is also working full time. We are grateful for the continuing support of our families: Tom, Patrick, Brian-Martin, and Tomás Samway, Chris Dobie, and Norm, Daniel, and Karl Gusner. It would have been very difficult to write this book if they had not been interested in its progress. We are indebted to Norm and Tom for the way they listened sympathetically and knowledgeably. It is hard not to succeed when surrounded by the kind of pride and constant encouragement that we received from them. We are particularly grateful to Tom for the relaxing and interesting conversations and hot cups of coffee that preceded most of our work sessions, and to Norm for the wonderful meals that greeted Gail on her return home after long work sessions.

Note to Readers

This book describes literature study circles (LSCs) in Gail Whang's fifth/sixth grade classroom. The narration encompasses three perspectives: those of Gail as the classroom teacher; Katharine as the participant-observer-teacher; and both of us as collaborators. We have included this range of perspectives so as to capture more accurately what happened. This is primarily a story of children participating in literature study circles, but it is also the story of our collaboration.

Although we refer in this book to many children's and young adult books, readers will notice that we often bring up one book in particular, Linda Crew's *Children of the River*. Gail's students discussed this book frequently. We found it to be very popular with a wide range of students, both boys and girls, and children from diverse cultural backgrounds. Our experiences with this one book remind us of how powerful books can be when readers are completely hooked.

We refer to over sixty students, children we worked with over our four-year collaboration in the classroom. We present the language of the children exactly as they spoke or wrote. Many of the students are non-native English speakers, and this is sometimes reflected in the samples that we include. Because the writing that the students engaged in for LSCs was reflective and designed to help them prepare for discussions, all of the writing samples we include are first drafts. Revising or editing was unnecessary, as the writing was not intended for an audience other than the writers themselves.

Chapter 1

"I Gotta Read It!" Literature Study Circles in Action

INSIDE Gail Whang's fifth/sixth grade classroom the students are settling down after morning recess. They take books and reading logs out of their desks. "Have you read this?" María asks her neighbor, Graciela. She is referring to the book that she selected a few days earlier for literature study circles (LSCs), *Children of the River* by Linda Crew, about a Cambodian girl who flees her homeland, endures incredible hardships, and eventually settles in Oregon, where she encounters prejudice, cultural dissonance—and love with Jonathan, the star player on the football team. Graciela shakes her head and says, "No, pero lo leyó Angelina" (No, but Angelina read it). The two girls, both Latinas, giggle a little as they look at the covers and flip through the pages of their respective books, talking about them. Across the oblong table is Eric, who has begun to read *There's a Bat in Bunk Five* (Danziger). He glances across at the two girls and says, "I read that before Easter. It's good." The three students talk a little about *Children of the River*—how popular it is with their class, how it has a love story, and how sad it is in parts. As if to validate their comments about the moving qualities of the story, María says, "Ms. Whang say she cried when she read it." Graciela raises her eyebrows as if astonished. "I gotta read it!" she announces.

At this point, Gail asks the *Children of the River* group to join her on the rug. María leaves her table and joins four other students on the worn brown rug that is host to many classroom events, including whole class discussions, writing conferences, and literature study circle discussions. The rest of the class is either reading or writing in literature logs. A pleasant, purposeful quiet pervades the room, punctuated from time to time by brief conversations and students getting up for a drink of water or to browse in the classroom library. Gail is on her way to the rug, but is waylaid by Jason, who has left his book at home. When she joins the group a couple of minutes later, the four girls (Rosa, María, Angelina, and Sylvia) and one boy (Jarvis) are already engaged in a vigorous discussion. Jarvis and Rosa make room between them for Gail. She sits down and listens to their conversation, which tumbles out, one person interrupting and building upon the comments of another. It is clear that they have been very taken by this book:

ROSA: In the beginning of the book it make me cry because, um, there was, they had a war so they had to leave. And when the baby died, it make me cry, too.

ANGELINA: Yeah. It made me cry, too.

ROSA (*interrupting Angelina*): It was a really good book. I really enjoy it. Like when I was reading it my mom said, like, "Rosa, put the book down!" "No, it's too good to put it down." "So you've gotta go to bed." "I don't wanna go to bed. I wanna finish it all up."

ANGELINA: It was good. I like the part—it was scary, the part where the baby dies.

The students talk about how Sundara, the main character, thinks a doll she finds in a junkyard is the baby that died on the boat in which she escaped from Cambodia. They are animated as they talk, using gestures and sounds to emphasize Sundara's emotional reaction, and spontaneously reading aloud sections from the book that moved them. Sometimes the students' comments spill out so quickly that at first it sounds as if they may not be listening to each other. But if one listens and watches carefully, it becomes clear that they are listening to each other; their comments often refer back to points others have made, and they frequently indicate agreement (for example, "Yeah, that was the part I like, too").

At first Gail simply listens to the students, figuring out the direction of the conversation and the issues that are important to them. On occasion, she attempts to interject a comment; but the students are immersed in their topic, and she has to work as hard as the other group members to make her voice heard. What is striking is that this type of dynamic group discussion is rarely seen in classrooms, where teacher talk often dominates classroom discourse. In effect, Gail is seen by the students as just one member of the group rather than as the authority figure.

The conversation continues to explore a variety of issues—the love story involving Sundara and Jonathan, events on the boat coming from Cambodia, and family relationships. At one point in the conversation, the discussion focuses on cultural differences and stereotypes:

ROSA: Look at this one. Look at this one. See, the thing I didn't like. Aunt Soka was, she was unfair with Sundara. Sundara always took good grades and all that, but then Aunt Soka—

ANGELINA (*interrupting*): Yeah. And she said, "You don't have enough time to have relationships."

SYLVIA: I thought that was the one, um—

ROSA (*interrupting*): There was, there was. Right here, in the book, there was a stereotype. Did you notice that? Besides (*inaudible*). . .

JARVIS: When she went in the coach's office, it was a stereotype.

(*A lot of students are speaking at the same time.*)

GAIL: Wait, wait, let Rosa finish. Go ahead.

ROSA: It was a stereotype because her aunty didn't want her to, to go out with people.

SYLVIA (*speaking over Rosa*): Go out with people.

ANGELINA: Because they were mean. Because they were racism.

SYLVIA: And her culture.

(*Several students are speaking together.*)

GAIL: Wait. Wait. You'll all get a chance to speak. (*Lots of laughter and giggles.*) This is very exciting that you like the book, but hold that thought, Angelina. Go ahead [Rosa] and finish. So what was the stereotype that she had?

ROSA: Her aunty didn't want her to go out with white people, what she didn't like. And the other people didn't really like to, didn't really talk to Sundara because she was Cambodian. And only Jonathan talked to her.

The group then explores how difficult it must have been for Sundara, who was now a member of two cultures, Cambodian and American. The students personalize the pronouns, substituting "we're" for "they're." It appears that they are talking for Sundara. Their comments suggest that they identify with Sundara, perhaps reflecting the fact that each of them may encounter similar cross-cultural difficulties, as they are all first- or second-generation Latinos (Rosa, María, Angelina, and Sylvia) or Filipino/African American (Jarvis). As they talk, they negotiate what they mean by such terms as "peer pressure" and "family pressure":

SYLVIA: I thought it was difficult for Sundara to be both Cambodian and American because when she was at home, we're—

ANGELINA (*completing Sylvia's idea*): aren't American but are Cambodians.

SYLVIA (*interrupting*): I know. We're not more American, we're Cambodian. You're supposed to do what our culture does. And when she's at school, she's all, Jonathan's all, "Come on, go out with me." She's all, "Huh?" She's all, pressure. Going home they tell her, no. At school, yeah. No, yeah, no, yeah. Aaaaaaah!

GAIL: So you felt like it was difficult to go between two cultures?

ANGELINA: To develop. When people are pressuring you, it's hard to develop or to get ideas because you're like, should I? Shouldn't I? Should I? Shouldn't I?

GAIL (*speaking over Angelina*): Uh-huh.

ANGELINA (*breaking in*): You stay in the same place. You don't like, go high, you don't study because you're thinking what should you do. Should you be American or should you be Chinese. Or, I mean Cambodian.

SYLVIA: That's peer pressure.

GAIL: It's peer pressure. What do you mean by that?

ANGELINA: No, that's family pressure.

SYLVIA: No, it ain't.

ROSA: Family pressure.

SYLVIA: Well, sort of peer pressure. Like they're making her do something she really doesn't want to do.

JARVIS: Yup.

GAIL: Well, let's just talk about this for a minute, OK? (*Students giggle and continue to talk over each other.*) Wait, could we just finish this discussion because there's so many different ideas that you're talking about. This is great. So what kind of pressure was she feeling from the family then?

ANGELINA: That she should be Cambodian. That she should, that she should—

ROSA: —follow the tradition. Like Moni (*another character in the book*).

ANGELINA: Follow the tradition and let her parents choose, choose her husband.

SYLVIA: That wasn't fair.

ANGELINA: I know. That is totally unfair. 'Cause, 'cause they're gonna (*students all talk together*)—

GAIL: Wait, Rosa, wait. Let her finish.

ANGELINA: When I'm twenty years old. When I'm twenty-one years old. OK, they're gonna say you're gonna, you're gonna, you're gonna marry this guy and then at the wedding I'm finally gonna meet him for the *first* time in my life, I'm gonna meet my husband.

SYLVIA: That's dumb.

ANGELINA: And then what if you don't like it? What if you don't like the person?

ROSA: I know, really.

SYLVIA: I mean, uuugh! That's unfair, huh?

GAIL: So you don't like that part of the Cambodian culture—(*interrupted by students talking all together*).

SYLVIA: Who could ever marry someone without knowing them or without loving them?

JARVIS: Yeah.

ROSA: I think that it isn't right, that wasn't fair, like choosing on your husband, 'cause it matters how you feel on the inside, not out, not how your parents feel.

SYLVIA: Yeah.

ROSA: It's not like they gonna marry him. It's *you* gonna marry. It's your (*inaudible*) happy. It's not their life.

ANGELINA: (*inaudible*) the hard tradition to her was controlling her life or letting her parents control her. That was a hard decision because, because if she didn't obey her aunt and her uncle, she would be kicked out. They would kick her out and where would she live?

JARVIS: They would disown her.

ANGELINA: They would kick her out. They would kick her out and where would she live? She *had* to obey them 'cause if she didn't then she'd get kicked out and if she did she wouldn't live happy for the rest of her life. So both ways she end up losing.

SYLVIA: But at the last part she, her aunty understood.

The part of the conversation that touches on arranged marriages is particularly evocative for Gail, as her grandmother came from Korea to the United States as a "picture bride." The marriage had been arranged by friends of the family, and the couple lived together for over fifty years. Gail waits for a moment to share this information with the group, but the conversation swirls around and she realizes that she may have to wait until later.

Later in the discussion, the group continues to explore Cambodian customs, grounding their comments in prior knowledge, challenging the accuracy of each other's statements, and clarifying meaning as they proceed.

SYLVIA: OK, OK. I thought it was sad about the baby, but I thought the funny part was when the lady said, "Oh please let the baby live. I promise to shave all my hairs." When the baby was, when they were gonna throw it—

ANGELINA: Overboard.

SYLVIA: Overboard. She's all saying, "Oh, please let the baby live. I promise to do anything. I promise to shave my legs."

JARVIS: She prays.

MARÍA: Shave her legs?

SYLVIA: No. What is, why is she gonna promise?

JARVIS: Then she was saying, "I pray to God that my baby lives" and stuff.

ROSA (*speaking over Jarvis*): Uh-uh. I think they say—

MARÍA (*reading from the book, correcting miscues as she reads*): "She would pray to God, promise to have, to shave all her long hair and gradually (in gratitude) if only the child would live."

JARVIS: And she take her life, to give her life to let the baby live and stuff.

ROSA: The Cambodian people shave their face. Did you know that?

SYLVIA: Her face?

JARVIS: Their eyebrows, too?

ROSA: Their eyebrows, their face,

SYLVIA: Aagh!

ROSA: Their arms and their heads too. Didn't you know that?

JARVIS: Their head too?

ANGELINA: Yeah, what do you think about a woman that are Cambodian don't have eyebrows. They put makeup on it. They put brown makeup and they go (*makes a slurping sound*).

SYLVIA: Ooah.

ANGELINA: Yeah, then she make a—then they have this little mark on the eye that goes like this (*makes a soft whipping sound*).

SYLVIA: Como (like) Bibi Gaetan (*referring to a Mexican singer and actress*). Like Bibi Gaetan. She makes those. Those are not hers.

ANGELINA: She paints them.

SYLVIA: I know.

JARVIS: Who?

SYLVIA: This um, this um—

ROSA: Mexican (*inaudible*)

ANGELINA: She's Mexican, um, actress.

SYLVIA: Yeah, she's all (*inaudible*) with big ass lips. And she goes (*inaudible*)

ANGELINA: I know and she's all—

SYLVIA (*interrupting*): Big lips and she does, um, she does double lips, she goes (*makes a revving sound*).

GAIL: With her lipstick?

SYLVIA: Yeah.

(*Laughter*)

During this exchange, Gail is silent. She wants to find out what the students know about Cambodian customs. She isn't quite sure herself about the details of the shaving custom, but suspects that Rosa and Angelina may have incomplete or inaccurate information. She decides to let the conversation follow its natural course and ask a Cambodian instructional aide about the custom at lunchtime. (Later, Gail learns that shaving isn't an intrinsic part of Cambodian culture. Some women—not all—shave off their eyebrows and draw them in with a pencil, as women in many countries do. Gail shared this information with the students later.)

As teachers, we often find ourselves in the awkward situation of asking questions or making comments only to be met with complete silence and blank stares. It is, therefore, exciting when students are so engaged in the conversation that we find it hard to get a word in edgeways. We know that passionate discussions that involve negotiating meaning, clarifying and justifying points of view, and drawing upon personal experience are too important for us to impose our own agendas, even those that evolve in the course of the discussion. We respect the students' insights, learn from them, and use them to guide us as teachers. In the conversation in Gail's classroom, Gail tries repeatedly to add her own insights and reactions to *Children of the River*. Eventually she is given "permission" by the group to comment. Immediately, however, her brief comment sparks further student input, and she is interrupted:

GAIL: Can I talk?

ANGELINA: Go ahead.

STUDENTS: Yeah. (*Laughter*)

SYLVIA: Yes, go ahead!

GAIL: No, I love this book too and, um—

ANGELINA (*interrupting*): I wanna buy it.

JARVIS: It was the best books since (*inaudible*)

SYLVIA (*interrupting*): Where'd you buy this book, anyway?

ANGELINA: Yeah, where can we buy it?

ROSA: Yeah, where can we buy it, Ms. Whang, 'cause I really want to buy it.

ANGELINA: I really want to buy it and keep it.

GAIL: Really? (*Students respond affirmatively with "uums."*) Uh-huh. Why do you? Why?

ANGELINA: I just love it! (*Students all talk together, agreeing with Angelina.*)

JARVIS: 'Cause it's romantic.

ANGELINA: I want it continuing. I'd buy it. I mean, I just, I just feel like keeping it and reading it over and over and over.

GAIL: What's the reason that you want to do that? I mean—

ROSA (*interrupting*): The reason I want to buy it is because like every time, like every time I opened every single page it got me hooked up every single time and I didn't really want to put it down. Ms. Whang, I want to keep this book, you know. (*Students are all talking together.*)

GAIL: Yeah. You know what we could do, though? I could, um. It looks like it costs—

SYLVIA: Buy them?

ANGELINA: We could give you the money.

GAIL: Yeah. It costs three-fifty. So if you gave me, like—

ANGELINA (*interrupting*): OK. I'll bring my money probably on Friday. I'll bring my money on Friday.

GAIL (*trying to continue*): —Three-fifty, and I collect the money and I can just buy it for you. But what I want to know is, what is it that you would go back to read it for? What is it that—

SYLVIA (*interrupting*): All the part when she got in love with Jonathan. Aaaaaah.

ANGELINA: And then, in the beginning, in the beginning chapters because it explains how they felt. How they felt when they were running away, when they were moving her place to place because people were coming and killing them and then it was really sad because she never got to see her parents. She never ever got to see her parents over.

A little later, Jarvis mentions how the book reminded him of when he and his brothers and mother ran away from his father. The rest of the group does not respond to Jarvis's intensely personal comment, except to listen respectfully to him. They move on to discuss why they think Linda Crew named her book *Children of the River*. They talk more about the cross-cultural difficulties that Sundara experienced. They talk about relationships between various characters in the book, and the depth of the relationships. They talk more about how the book affected them. They talk about how the book hooked them utterly, completely, and surprisingly, as it was such a long book with very small type.

At the end of the discussion, which lasted about thirty minutes, Gail reviews the issues discussed and talks about assignments that the group members are to complete before they meet for a second discussion the following day. These assignments are not prearranged. Instead, they evolve out of the discussion and encourage the students to return to the book and look at elements of it more closely:

GAIL: One assignment is: Let's look at this question about going between two cultures, OK? And find how she—just that whole idea of how Sundara was in conflict, that sometimes she—
SYLVIA (*interrupting*): When it was difficult for her to go through both?
GAIL: Yeah, both cultures. Being American and being Cambodian.
JARVIS: I betcha it was hard.

The group briefly clarifies the assignment and writes it down. Gail then asks them to also take a look at another issue:

GAIL: I'm going to give you another assignment, too. I want to know three places where you really felt emotional. Where she [Linda Crew] really brought out your own feelings of emotion. You were saying this book is so emotional and it made you cry. You were sad, you were angry, you were scared. Find three places that really—
ANGELINA (*interrupting*): Hooked you.
GAIL: That really hooked you. Where you experienced strong feelings.
ANGELINA: When you started thinking about it.

Before the group leaves to join the rest of the class, they quickly debrief:

GAIL: Before you go, tell me what you thought about this discussion.
STUDENTS: I loved it. Perfect. It was great.
ROSA: We all share our feelings.
ANGELINA: I would like to be in this (*inaudible*) for the rest of my life. Just reading and reading and reading.
SYLVIA: Hey, Ms. Whang, why don't you always give us books—
JARVIS (*finishing the thought*): Like this.
ANGELINA: Do you have any more books like these, of Linda Crew?
SYLVIA (*breaking in*): Linda Crew, all of them.
ANGELINA: Please, more.
GAIL: Well, I don't know if she's written any more, but we can check. That's the other thing you can—
JARVIS (*interrupting*): She should get an award for this.
ROSA: Here it says. Lookit. It says, "A 1990 Golden Ki." (*Rosa is reading*

from the back cover, where it indicates that the book has won several awards, including the 1990 Golden Kite Award from the Society of Children's Book Writers.)

The students continue their discussion of the book as they return to their tables in the main part of the classroom.

Gail crosses the room to talk briefly with Katharine, who regularly visits the classroom. At lunchtime, we talk about how *Children of the River* has been very popular with so many fifth and sixth grade girls and boys from different linguistic and cultural backgrounds. It thoroughly captures the students' imaginations, minds, and hearts. It engenders the kind of engagement with a book that teachers dream of. Neither of us is sure why this particular book has had such a powerful effect.

On the following day, when the class gets together after the morning recess, the same group of students meets with Gail for a follow-up discussion. Their copies of the book are strewn with scraps of paper on which they have written brief comments in response to their assignment of the day before. They briefly confirm that they have all focused on the same topics and immediately launch into a conversation about where the book hooked them:

ROSA: Okay, on page 159, I got hooked when he says, "I love you." And he goes, "Ask me a question I could answer. Ask me if I love you."

ANGELINA (*breaking in*): Yeah. And I also got hooked.

(*Students talk together.*)

GAIL: Wait. Why don't—Let's all share one at a time.

ANGELINA: I got hooked right from the beginning when there were, um, running away from the, um, uh, what's their name?

ROSA: Soldiers.

ANGELINA: From the soldiers. That got me hooked. And the baby, she was really sick and she was all (*makes a choking sound*).

GAIL: Can you find a page? Was there a specific page?

ANGELINA (*breaking in*): No. It was right in the first chapter.

GAIL: Uh-huh. What about that hooked you?

ANGELINA: The way that she explained it. The way that, it just vibrated me.

Angelina's comment that the writing "vibrated" her is very telling. Clearly, this book resonates with the students. But just what is it that Linda Crew does as an author to captivate these readers? Is it the actions or the words of the characters? Is it the love story? There's no question that the love theme captivated the students. They identify with the main character, Sundara, and her struggles, and are curious about how the cross-cultural romance would play itself out, as the following excerpt indicates:

MARÍA: Um. I think I said it already . . . when, um, he showed her the picture. Yeah, and then, um, he's like, "You look cute" (*interrupted by another student, making her inaudible*). . . . Are they gonna kiss, or what? I was like, what's gonna happen? You know, and I was like (*inaudible*). . .

GAIL: So you like the romance?

STUDENTS: Yeah.

This follow-up discussion is an opportunity for readers to revisit the book and continue to explore it, as well as an occasion for them to become more conscious of the writer's craft. It is, of course, hard for any of us to put our finger on the literary elements that hook us as readers, but it is clear from the discussion in Gail's classroom that even though the students may not have the vocabulary to express themselves succinctly, they are able to talk about these elements. The students were hooked by the description of emotions, the theme, the plot elements, and the romance.

As these excerpts from two LSCs focusing on *Children of the River* illustrate, the students explored many issues that were important to them: family strife, flight from war, adjustment to life in a new culture, and prejudice are just a few issues that they discussed. The students reveled in the book and in the open-ended discussions that allowed them to follow their conversational inclinations. Occasionally someone did not completely understand the sequence of events in the story and the group discussion helped to resolve the difficulties. Gail did not need to check on comprehension, as the students' conversation revealed the degree to which they had understood the book. Through LSCs, the students had a chance to enjoy a book while they explored critical issues they may confront in their own lives. In their previous school experiences, they had not always had such opportunities to become absorbed in books.

The School, the Students, and Their Neighborhood

Although it is July, Jarvis, María, Rosa, Angelina, and Sylvia are still in school, along with over one thousand other students (three-quarters of the total school population). They attend Hawthorne Year-Round Elementary School, a year-round, multitrack school. As the numbers suggest, this is a huge school. It is located in the middle of a multiethnic neighborhood in the inner city of Oakland, one of California's largest cities. What is now one school used to be three—there are three distinct school buildings and several portables on the school campus. Hawthorne is located in a low-income neighborhood that is home to many ethnic and immigrant groups. Around Hawthorne live many African Americans, a few European Americans and Native Americans, and many first- and second-generation immigrants from Cambodia, El Salvador, Guatemala, Laos, Mexico, Nicaragua, the Philippines, and Vietnam.

Because the Hawthorne neighborhood is home to immigrants from Asia and Latin America, many of the students are acquiring English as a nonnative language. Some of the classes are designated as bilingual, and teachers provide instruction in both English and Spanish. Other classes, however, have students who speak a variety of native languages, and the shared language is English. In these cases, the teachers have received preparation in how to work with students who are acquiring English as a nonnative language. Gail is one of these teachers.

Gail's fifth/sixth multiage class of thirty students is ethnically mixed. Some students were born in the United States (African Americans, Asian Americans, European Americans, Latino Americans, and Native Americans). Others are immigrants (from Burma, Cambodia, El Salvador, Fiji, Guatemala, Laos, Mexico, the Philippines, and Vietnam). Still others are immigrants who were not born in their family's homeland (Laotian and Mien students born in refugee camps in Thailand). English is the common language in the class, but a third of the students speak Spanish and almost a third speak Laotian. There is an equal number of boys and girls. (We refer to more than sixty students in the course of this book because we have included discussions and journal entries collected over four years.)

When listening to many of the students speaking, one often finds evidence of the fact that English is not their native language. It is not uncommon to hear articles omitted, verb tenses confused, and pronouns mixed up. Also, these students often seem to be searching for appropriate words. These are typical developmental miscues for second language learners. (We have transcribed the oral and written language of the students exactly as it occurred in order to better reflect the students and their achievements.)

When we first wrote about our experiences with literature study circles, we invited students to join us (see Samway et al. 1991). Our young co-authors asserted that we should include background information in order for adult readers, particularly teachers, to realize that a successful LSC program is possible in circumstances that often seem very difficult. As educators of and advocates for all students, particularly those for whom society often has low expectations (for example, inner-city students from low-income and/or immigrant backgrounds), we are constantly searching for effective ways to build upon and learn from the children's knowledge, experiences, interests, and special skills. We have come to realize that a well-designed language arts program that includes LSCs can do just that.

What Is a Literature Study Circle?

A great deal of attention has been paid to using children's literature as the basis for reading. Unlike most literature-based reading programs, literature study circles is an approach that emphasizes the reading and discussing of unabridged, unexcerpted children's literature in small, self-selected groups (see Bird and Alvarez 1987; Edelsky 1988; Eeds and Wells 1989; Peterson and Eeds 1990; Samway et al. 1991; Short and Pierce 1990; Smith 1990). It gives students choice over what they read. It assumes comprehension and relies heavily on open-ended discussions. In this book we describe only one way of approaching LSCs. Other teachers implement quite different LSCs—for example, students could meet for a book discussion without the teacher (Daniels 1994). In the LSCs we describe, the teacher is present and acts as both a knowledgeable reader and a mentor of learners.

In Gail's class, students select a new LSC book every week to ten days. On the day of the selection, Gail brings in six to eight copies each of four or five books. She selects these books based on the interests of her students and the degree to which she thinks they will lend themselves to discussion. (Appendix A lists some suitable titles for fifth and sixth graders.) She makes sure to include shorter or less complex texts so that students who are still emerging as readers in English can have a successful experience. Sometimes, though, these students choose a longer text. In these cases, their selections are often influenced by the choices of their friends, and they frequently read the book together.

After Gail has described each book briefly in a session called a book-talk, students select which book they will read; if too many students want the same book, a lottery system is used to decide who gets the book. The students are given large blocks of time in class to read. At the beginning of the year, less experienced readers tend to be able to read for no more than twenty minutes before getting restless; as they become more experienced readers and more familiar with LSCs, they can usually read comfortably for one hour. Students reading the same book determine how many pages they must read each day in order to finish the book by the due date, usually a week or ten days later, sooner if the book is very short. They read the entire book before getting together for a small group discussion (the LSC). On occasion, Gail checks in with groups of students or an individual student, just to make sure that they are on top of their reading and not struggling. Sometimes she meets with an entire group, usually when she discovers that the book is causing problems for several members of the group.

On the agreed-upon day, a book group meets with Gail for a twenty- to thirty-minute discussion in which all members share their initial reactions to the book. Based on this discussion, an assignment is generated that is intended to extend the students' understanding of the book and the craft of writing. For example, after a discussion about *The Cay* (T. Taylor), the group agreed to investigate how the author revealed changes in the young boy's character. Other assignments have considered such questions as "What does the author do to make you feel like you're there in the book?" and "What do you think is the theme of the book? Find clues to back up your answer." Each participant works on the assignment before returning to the group for a second session one or two days later.

The first LSC session is often devoted to personal, aesthetic responses to the literature (what readers liked about the book, what it made them think about). The second (and sometimes subsequent) session focuses more on an analysis of literary elements (for example, the development of plot, how an author reveals a character, the role of the narrator) in response to the assignment. Aesthetic response often continues, however, in this later session. All the participants, including Gail, come to the discussion with evidence to support their views. Differences are respected, but views must be supported. Gail takes the part of an informed and engaged equal participant in these discussions, and she encourages the students to talk with each other rather than to her. She is eager for a thoughtful, invigorating conversation rather than a simple display of knowledge.

At the end of each discussion, the group briefly reflects on how the session went. In this way, participants can evaluate their own and each other's contributions to the discussion and can explore the role of the group in gaining meaning. At these times the students and teacher are honest, but supportive of each other. While Gail is meeting with a group, the rest of the students are either reading quietly, writing in their literature logs, or doing the assignment for a follow-up session. (Chapter 2 discusses in greater detail how we implement and maintain LSCs.)

The Origin of LSCs

It is difficult, if not impossible, to discuss the theoretical underpinnings of LSCs because they were "invented" by fifth grade students over a decade ago. We are indebted to Karen Smith and her fifth grade students in Arizona for discovering and developing a way of approaching reading in schools that has changed our lives as teachers in profound ways. Although LSCs were not the brainchild of a theorist, they do have strong roots in theory. In essence, LSCs are grounded in a socio-psycholinguistic view of the reading process, one that recognizes the way in which reading is a meaning-making process. When encountering a text, readers bring their own life and literary experiences to it (for an overview of the related research, see Weaver 1994). That is, reading is a transactional process, one in which readers actively construct meaning with the print that is on the page based on their experiences and knowledge base. Louise Rosenblatt's reader response theory (1978, 1983, 1991) suggests that there are as many potential interpretations of a text as there are readers. In addition, Rosenblatt distinguishes between two ways of experiencing a text: reading for understanding ("efferent response") and reading as engagement with a text ("aesthetic response")—an idea that is central to LSCs.

Gail's Development as a Teacher

When Gail started teaching fifth and sixth grade about ten years ago, she used the basal textbook. She noticed how unengaged her students were, however, so in an effort to make reading more interesting, she introduced the idea of contracts for each textbook story so the students could be more independent. They would read a story, answer comprehension questions, define words, and do worksheets on the rules of grammar and punctuation. This enabled the students to work more independently, but their reactions continued to range from being utterly bored to hating reading.

Gail then wrote a small school district grant with Diana Metoyer, another fifth/sixth grade teacher. They requested class sets of Judy Blume books because they wanted students to become more engaged readers. They chose Judy Blume because they thought students would identify with the problems of growing up that Blume writes about and be able to relate to the characters in her books. With this approach, students got to read trade books as opposed to textbook stories, but they still had contracts to complete. In order to move from one chapter to the next, students had to complete their contracts (which included such activities as defining vocabulary, answering questions about the reading, drawing a picture, and doing independent assignments). The trade books were not part of the official reading program, however, and were scheduled for the afternoon so as not to disturb the regular reading program. The students enjoyed the books, but they hated having to stop at the end of each chapter. They moaned, "Do we have to do all this work?" Gail remembers thinking that she had to give them the assignments so as to ensure that they understood what they read.

Then, in 1989, after becoming more and more discouraged with the basal textbook, Gail totally abandoned it and decided to use only trade books. She received another small grant and bought class sets of several novels. Sometimes the whole class would read the same book. Other times, half the class would read one book while the other half read another. Gail would meet with half the class and they would have a discussion, the kind of discussion where the teacher fires questions at the students. They spent a lot of time reading aloud, round robin style, one student at a time. Gail wanted to make sure the students understood what they were reading; she thought that reading aloud was a way to establish this. She continued to use literature contracts.

Gail was elated. Many of the students loved the books. They wanted to read longer than the time allotted for reading. She faced a new dilemma, though, and remembers talking about it with a colleague: "These kids want to read the book, which is my goal, but I don't want them to get so far ahead of everybody else. What will they do if they finish the book and everybody else is still reading?" Although Gail felt badly that the eager students couldn't go ahead with their reading, she was convinced that they couldn't truly comprehend and appreciate the book unless they discussed the "important questions" that came after every chapter. It didn't occur to her to think of how she would react if she had to stop every fifteen minutes to discuss the meaning of an exciting book she was reading or a movie she was watching.

Around 1989, Gail met Katharine at a yearlong seminar for teachers. The seminar, led by Katharine, was devoted to literature study circles. Katharine had first encountered this approach at Fair Oaks School in the Redwood City School District in northern California. At the urging of the school's resource teacher, Gloria Norton, and a consultant, Lois Bird, the Fair Oaks teachers had been learning from Carole Edelsky of Arizona State University and Karen Smith (then an upper grade teacher in Arizona) about literature study circles, and they welcomed other teachers into their classrooms to observe and learn. Katharine had visited many classrooms in her role as a teacher-educator, but she had rarely encountered the high level of engagement that she observed in the Fair Oaks classrooms. Students from backgrounds similar to those of the students at Hawthorne School displayed a tremendous enthusiasm for books and book discussions. Rich conversations occurred. Students moved easily from reading in one language (usually English) to talking about the books in another language (usually Spanish, as many of the students were recent Latino immigrants to the United States). Katharine noticed how the students reveled in the open-ended discussions.

Katharine began to read all she could find on LSCs and the underlying theoretical perspectives. She also began to work with two elementary teachers who were interested in moving away from textbooks, albeit literature-based textbooks. With Barbara Schmidt and Kathy Maloney, Katharine began to implement LSCs and found that they were as successful in these Oakland classrooms as they had been in Redwood City. After a while, she began to introduce LSCs to other teachers, including Gail.

When Gail first heard about literature study circles, she was very interested because the approach seemed to answer many questions that she had pondered for years on how to make reading exciting and enjoyable for students. It made more sense to her than what she was currently doing as a teacher. Perhaps because her teacher preparation program did not include a single course in literacy development, Gail started her career at the whim of textbook publishers and writers of ill-informed curricula guides. She had to rely on her own instincts and informal learning in order to become a more knowledgeable and satisfied teacher. But she still focused on activities. Only recently has Gail begun to question what reading is and how, as a teacher, she can build on the natural capacity of children to actively make sense of texts, alone and collaboratively.

We have now worked together with LSCs for four years. In that time, we have seen how changed once-reluctant readers can become when given choices, time to read in school, and opportunities to talk about books with others. Although we do not believe that there is only one way to implement LSCs, in Chapter 2 we present the way we have done it and address issues we have found to be critical in ensuring a successful program.

Many of the students with whom Gail works have not had much success in the past as readers. Generally speaking, they have been exposed to textbook- and worksheet-based approaches to reading and have been given few opportunities to read books for enjoyment or information. We have been struck by the dramatic changes in the experiences and attitudes of these fifth and sixth grade students toward reading as a result of their engagement in LSCs. In Chapter 3 we explore these changes—how these students have come to view themselves as readers.

LSCs can lead to increased cross-cultural understanding. This was not something we anticipated when we first started working with them. Instead, the idea emerged as we participated in LSCs and read transcripts of discussions. We have been moved by the honesty of students as they have talked about difficult issues that are important to them. We have been impressed with the power of literature (and open-ended discussions) to bring people together who might otherwise misunderstand and distrust each other. In Chapter 4, we explore the influence LSCs can have on cross-cultural understanding.

Educators are beginning to realize that teaching is not a static endeavor with a discrete body of skills, information, or attributes. Nowadays, the professional literature emphasizes how teaching is a process of lifelong learning. When we first started to write this book, we wondered if we were being presumptuous. As we observe and listen to children engaging in LSCs and other literacy events, as we talk with colleagues, and as we read the professional literature, we are reminded that we have lots of questions. We look forward to finding answers to these questions— and to generating new questions. We have always appreciated the courage of other teachers who have offered an honest view of their practice, including its false starts, uncertainties, and low points. We have tried to follow in their footsteps, particularly in Chapter 5, where we discuss some of the questions we have and new directions in which we would like to go.

 # Chapter 2

"What Did You Think of the Book?" Getting LSCs Off the Ground

O NE DAY, Katharine enters Gail's fifth/sixth grade classroom and glances around. Although the end-of-recess bell sounded only a few minutes earlier, a purposeful quiet pervades the room. Some of the children glance up as she comes in and sits at the round table by the door. One student sitting at a nearby table waves and calls out, "Hi," but most of the students appear unaware that she has entered, focused as they are on what they are doing. Several are reading, some at their clusters of desks, some on pillows on the rug. Others are writing in notebooks. Two students are browsing in the class library, flipping through the pages of books; occasionally one student hands over a book for the other to look at. After a couple of minutes, Gail asks the students who have read *The Cat Ate My Gymsuit* (Danziger) to meet her on the rug. Seven students join her on the rug; two other students who are already sitting there pick up their pillows and move to the outskirts of the rug, where they resume their reading.

An animated discussion ensues as the group discusses the book. They begin by talking about the parts of the book and the characters they liked best. They compare Gail to Ms. Phinney, the teacher in the book who stood by her principles, in the process losing her job. One student connects events in the book to the conflict resolution program at the school when she says, "The father of Marcy wasn't good to her. He never gave her a chance, like in conflict management." Most of the discussion, however, focuses on the theme of the book, censorship, the Pledge of Allegiance, and whether there is really liberty and justice for all. At the end of the discussion, Gail briefly reviews the issues they have discussed and then asks the students to prepare for a follow-up discussion the next day by thinking about two things: Ms. Phinney not returning to school and whether that was fair; and freedom of speech and whether people have the right to say whatever they want. As the students leave the rug and return to their desks, they are already animatedly discussing this second issue.

For the thirty minutes or so that these seven students and Gail are meeting to discuss *The Cat Ate My Gymsuit,* the rest of the class is working independently. From time to time, students glance up from their reading, writing, or thinking, and appear to be listening to the discussion. From the spot where Gail is sitting in the circle on the rug, she can see the rest of the class. Although her goal is to give her undivided attention to the group discussion, she realizes that she needs to be aware of what is going on in other parts of the room. At one point she notices that Somphone and Sonenalinh are talking and laughing while glancing toward the window that overlooks the school yard. She is concerned that they may be distracting other students. She is also concerned that they may not be using their time wisely. Although she can't hear their conversation clearly, she suspects that it is probably unrelated to the books they are supposed to be reading and calls out, "Somphone and Sonenalinh." The two boys turn, look at Gail, and return to their reading.

After the students reading *The Cat Ate My Gymsuit* return to their desks, some begin working on their assignment. A couple of students put off their assignment and pull out another book to read. Gail crosses the room and slides into an empty desk next to Peter, a newcomer to the school, who selected *Mississippi Bridge* (M. Taylor) for LSCs. She decides to have a quick reading conference with him, as she suspects that Peter is struggling with his reading. She noticed that he had been gazing around the room, seemingly disengaged from the book. She wants to check in with him to see if he needs help. She wants him to have a successful experience with the book and be ready for the discussion. Because Gail has learned that all students enjoy the book discussions and look forward to them, she wants to make sure that Peter is ready to contribute, which he is unlikely to be able to do if he hasn't finished the book.

GAIL: How's it going, Peter?
PETER: Fine.
GAIL: Tell me about the book.
PETER: Well, it's kinda hard.
GAIL: Why don't you read a little to me?
PETER: OK.

Peter reads from page eight, focusing on every word, trying to sound them out. Gail makes a mental note that she needs to spend time with him teaching him reading strategies that focus on making meaning (for example, pausing frequently to ask yourself whether what you are reading makes sense; reading on to see if you can draw meaning from the context). For the moment, however, she decides to encourage Peter's having a good experience with this particular book and asks him if he would like to read the book with someone else. He nods yes. As he has barely begun the book, Gail asks Peter if he would like her to begin reading from the beginning. Again he nods. As she spends ten minutes or so reading the book, Peter frequently interjects comments indicating that he understands the plot and is interested in the story. As Gail reads aloud and talks with Peter about the book, she tries to figure out who can regularly read with him. She does not have time to read to a single student very often. A couple of options pop into her head: one of the other students who is reading the same book or an adult volunteer who comes into the class three days a week. After finishing the short read-aloud and talking a little about the book, Gail asks Peter if he would like to continue reading the book with someone else. He says that he would, but hesitates when Gail suggests that a peer read to him. They agree that Ginger, the adult volunteer, will read with him.

As Gail leaves Peter's desk, Kadedra calls to her, "Ms. Whang, come here. Did Winnie drink the water? Phonesavanh said she did. I didn't get what happened at the end." Kadedra is reading *Tuck Everlasting* (Babbitt); it's not unusual for students to be divided in their opinion about whether the young girl, Winnie, elects to drink the magic water that could give her eternal life. When students are having difficulty understanding a book, we usually meet very briefly with that group to help them get on track. In this case, however, Kadedra has already finished the book and the group will be meeting the next day, so Gail suggests to Kadedra that she take another look at that part of the book and write in her literature log what she thinks happened with Winnie. Gail reminds Kadedra that they will be talking about the book the next day and suggests that Kadedra raise this issue in the discussion.

Several children in the class are acquiring English as a nonnative language. Gail wants to check in with them also, so she moves around the room from one cluster of desks to another. She stops by Fahm and May Phou, both native Mien speakers who are orally fairly fluent in English, but who have a great deal of difficulty when reading and writing. They tell Gail that they have been having a hard time with *The Hundred Dresses* (Estes), a longer picture book. It turns out, however, that they have independently resolved their problem by pairing up and reading the book together. When Gail asks them to tell her about the book, it is clear that they understand it, even though there may be some words or concepts with which they are not familiar. Viliphone and Malcolm are sitting at the same cluster of desks with Fahm and May Phou. Both have already finished their LSC books and are reading other chapter books. Viliphone is totally engrossed in her new book, *Yellow Bird and Me* (Hansen). Earlier that morning, she told Gail that she selected this book because she enjoyed *The Gift-Giver* (Hansen), which she had read a couple of weeks ago for LSCs. Malcolm looks up as Gail talks with Fahm and May Phou, listens for a moment, and returns to his nonfiction book about mammals. While talking with the nonnative English speakers, Gail touches base with other students, too. Through asking such questions as "What do you think of this book?" "Are you having any difficulties?" "What do you need to do in order to finish it by our meeting on Friday?" she is able to learn more about the students' reading processes, preferences, and difficulties.

Katharine had planned on staying for only fifteen or twenty minutes, but she ends up staying for almost an hour. She observes students quietly talking about books with other students ("You read this? What happen?") and making recommendations ("You should read this. It so sad!"). From time to time, students leave their places at the tables, desks, and rug to get a drink from the sink, chat briefly with other students, pick up their reading logs from the bins, or choose another book. When students aren't

---

Roll of Thunder, Hear My Cry

I think that this book is really a good example of being prejudice against Black people for eample where littel man his sister and brother go to school and when the white kids pass by the Black kids get splashed by the mud and the white kids don't get in trouble for that I think that is awfully not fair. I am shure glad that they got their revenge by digging a hole so they could crash in it and guess what they did and they had to walk all the way and specially the girls they were complaining alot about getting dirty with their fancy dresses and their shiny shoes. What I also though that was really mean was when those American kids gave the Black people those used beat up math books and in the back it showed how many times the white kids used them and they gave them to the black kids when they were all torn apart and the pages were missing and they were also very dirty, that was very awfull.

Figure 1 A student's literature log entry

reading, they are usually writing in their literature logs, a place for them to record the titles and authors of books they've read. They also write their reactions to books (see Figure 1). Katharine is struck by how engaged with books and literacy acts these students are and by how long they remain engaged. As a teacher-educator, she has visited many classrooms and has rarely seen this level of engagement. It is true that not all the children are equally absorbed in their books during this hour explicitly devoted to reading. In fact, Gregory and Muey Seng are gazing around and rarely turn a page. But overall, there is a great deal of literate activity going on, and students appear to be taking charge of their time.

It's almost lunchtime now, and the students start putting their books and logs away. The quiet that has characterized the room for the last hour is quickly replaced by a busy, purposeful level of noise as the students discuss what game they're going to play at lunchtime, who's going to bring out the Chinese jump rope (rubber bands tied together in a rope about ten to twelve feet long), and what the cafeteria is serving for lunch.

This comfortable, successful scenario did not happen overnight. It has evolved over several years as Gail has become increasingly aware of the reading process and has challenged herself to provide authentic opportu-

---

nities for her students to read and respond to literature. Gail doesn't think that she has the answer; in fact, she is continually revising how she views LSCs and their role in a reading program (see Chapter 5). However, since she has been using LSCs she has seen and heard children who have never before enjoyed reading express tremendous excitement over books.

Two criteria that separate LSCs from many other literature-based reading approaches are that students have choice over what they read and book discussions are open-ended. However, simply offering book choices and opportunities to discuss books is just the beginning of a successful LSC program.

We have friends and colleagues who have introduced their students to LSCs after talking with us or taking part in one. They are excited and want to share that excitement with their students, but sometimes things don't work out quite the way they hoped. In some cases, teachers abandon the approach after a short time because they find that while they are leading an LSC, chaos reigns in the rest of the classroom. In other cases, teachers don't immediately have access to multiple copies of enough titles. Some are intimidated by the notion of inviting nonfluent readers to read independently. Also, some teachers are not very familiar with children's and young adult literature and do not feel confident that they can lead LSCs. In the case of new teachers who became familiar with LSCs in their teacher preparation programs, they often do not feel confident about using trade books when the rest of the faculty is using a reading series. Other teachers are reluctant to start LSCs because they believe that checking comprehension is important and they are not convinced that students can read independently and gain meaning without continual support from a teacher. Many teachers start with good intentions but don't have the support to help them work through the problems that can occur when implementing LSCs—for example, what to do with students who finish a book very quickly, what to do with students who don't finish in time for the discussion, how to manage the rotation of books, and how to handle students not getting their first choice of book.

Things didn't always go smoothly for Gail. Initially, she embraced LSCs simply because it seemed an interesting and fun activity for students. Her adoption of LSCs was not grounded in a different or deeper understanding of the reading process. It was only after she saw students reacting to the books, expressing strong opinions about what they read, and sharing their own life experiences as it related to the texts they read that Gail began to understand that reading is an active, transactional process (Rosenblatt 1983). Gail had many of the same questions that other teachers ask us, and in this chapter we would like to share ways in which we have addressed them.

Gail's Approach

Every week to ten days, Gail introduces her class to the current LSC book selection, usually four titles. After a brief "booktalk" of around ten minutes, during which Gail briefly describes each book, students make their choice by raising their hands as Gail calls out each title. As there are only eight copies of each book available, sometimes more students want to read a book than there are copies. In these situations, some students end up with their second or third choice. Gail makes a note of this so that the next time the class selects LSC books, these students will be sure to get their first choice. Once all the students have their books, Gail meets briefly with each group to agree on a date when they will meet for a first discussion. Books have to have been read in their entirety by that date. She reminds students that they will have time in class (up to an hour each day) and at home to read their books. Particularly at the beginning of the year, Gail brings in books that vary in length; this allows her to stagger the discussions. After about three days, the LSCs begin. These twenty-to thirty-minute discussions give students a chance to share their initial reactions to the book. Gail takes the part of an informed and engaged co-participant and shares her own responses to the book. When students are new to LSCs and unaccustomed to the format of the discussions, she begins with a simple, but open-ended question, such as "What did you think about the book?"

At the end of the first discussion, Gail paraphrases the conversation and then suggests a follow-up assignment grounded in the discussion. Because she wants students to look at the writer's craft and gain a deeper understanding of the book, these assignments usually require readers to go back and look more carefully at the book (for example, with such questions as How does the author show excitement? How does the author show the main character moving between two cultures?). The discussion closes with the group reflecting on what they have learned and their assessment of how well the session went. One or two days later, the same group meets with Gail for a follow-up session. Occasionally, students are so taken with a book that they want to continue exploring it in their groups; in these cases, additional meetings are scheduled.

With this format, over the course of a week to ten days Gail can meet with four or five groups at least twice. On some days she meets with two groups; on others she meets with only one group and spends the rest of the time conferring with students.

In the remainder of this chapter, we explore the issues that we have found to be important when implementing LSCs.

Selecting Books

Many of Gail's students do not have pleasant memories of books and reading. In fact, many say that they used to hate reading. Selecting books that are likely to engage students is critical and can lead to marked changes in how they view books and themselves as readers. When we have asked students to reflect upon LSCs, we often hear how the students have changed. Cheng writes:

> I remember last year I hated reading so much and I wouldn't want to read a book from beginning to the end. I think how my attitude change was because Ms. Whang helped me and my classmates by telling us how the book is and letting us be more curious in reading the book.

"Telling us how the book is" refers to Gail's description of the books in her introductory booktalks.

Quoc describes how the books themselves and the opportunity to talk about them changed his attitude toward reading:

> The beginning of this year I hated reading it was my worst subject in school. I thought it was boring. The middle of the year I like

reading a little bit but now I like it because Ms. Whang picks out
better books now and we have discussion too.

When we probe, we usually discover that in the past, reading involved
endless worksheets. Because many of Gail's students have been diagnosed
as poor readers, they have frequently received remedial reading instruction, which often relied on uninteresting, specially written books with
controlled language, worksheets that focused on discrete elements of written language (such as short vowels or digraphs), and unending lists of
questions about the texts. They have learned to believe that they are poor
readers; inevitably they regard reading as their least favorite subject. If
we are to help students get over these profoundly negative feelings about
books, it is critical that LSC books be selected very carefully. When we
do this, we take several factors into account.

Is the Book Likely to Be of Interest to the Students?

Students' current interests and concerns are important when making book
selections. Students enjoy humor, so *Matilda* (Dahl), *Ramona the Pest*
(Cleary), *Chocolate Fever* (R. K. Smith), *The War with Grandpa* (R. K.
Smith), *The Enormous Egg* (Butterworth), *Operation Dump the Chump*
(Park), and *Tales of a Fourth Grade Nothing* (Blume) have been popular
LSC selections. They also enjoy action; *All It Takes Is Practice* (Miles) and
Scorpions (Myers) have been popular. They like reading about dilemmas
facing young people; *The Cat Ate My Gymsuit* (Danziger), *Circle of Gold*
(Boyd), *Maniac Magee* (Spinelli), *Something to Count On* (Moore), *The
Shimmershine Queens* (Yarbrough), and *In the Year of the Boar and
Jackie Robinson* (Lord) have been successful choices. Clearly, they like
romance, as the popularity of *There's a Bat in Bunk Five* (Danziger) and
Children of the River (Crew) attests. They like reading about both their
own culture and cultures with which they come in contact, so they have
enjoyed *Lupita Mañana* (Beatty), *Roll of Thunder, Hear My Cry* (M.
Taylor), *Children of the River* (Crew), *In the Year of the Boar and Jackie
Robinson* (Lord), and *The Gift-Giver* (Hansen). They also like reading
books that are set in our geographic area, e.g., *Jar of Dreams* (Uchida),
Charlie Pippin (Boyd), and *Dragonwings* (Yep). Through class or small
group discussions, an issue may emerge that can lead to a deeper

discussion or unit of study. For example, after students had expressed concern over gang violence and peer pressure, Gail offered *Scorpions*, by Walter Dean Myers, as one of the choices for the next LSC.

Is the Book Likely to Lead to a Good Discussion?

When selecting books, we look for those with the potential for generating lively discussion. Books with one or more of the following have that potential:

- Rich language—for example, *Julie of the Wolves* (George), *The Whipping Boy* (Fleischman), and *Song of the Trees* (M. Taylor).

- Interesting plot—*Lupita Mañana* (Beatty), *Welcome Home, Jellybean* (Shyer), *Bunnicula* (Howe and Howe), and *Into the Dream* (Sleator).

- Richly developed characters—*The Great Gilly Hopkins* (Paterson), *Sadako and the Thousand Paper Cranes* (Coerr), and *A Taste of Blackberries* (D. B. Smith).

We also look for books with thought-provoking themes, such as:

- The pros and cons of eternal life—*Tuck Everlasting* (Babbitt).

- Racism—*Roll of Thunder, Hear My Cry* (M. Taylor), *Iggie's House* (Blume), *The Cay* (T. Taylor), and *Journey to Topaz* (Uchida).

- Homelessness—*Monkey Island* (Fox).

In our experience, the most successful books are those that leave readers with compelling questions about life, human relationships, or social issues.

Does the Book Seem Manageable to Students?

When introducing LSCs to a class containing less experienced or less fluent readers, it is wise to offer books that seem attainable in terms of length and size of print so that students have a successful first experience. We have found that reading shorter books—for example, *Song of the Trees* (M. Taylor), *Sadako and the Thousand Paper Cranes* (Coerr), *Fantastic Mr. Fox* (Dahl), *The Hundred-Penny Box* (Mathis), *The Real Thief* (Steig), *Molly's Pilgrim* (Cohen) or *The Hundred Dresses* (Estes)—can help get LSCs off the ground very effectively. If there are less fluent readers in the class or students who are in the process of learning English, shorter books with pictures can enhance understanding. *JT* (Wagner), a book with lots of photos, has been a particularly successful selection for less fluent readers. When Gregory, a struggling reader, completed reading *JT* on his own, he proudly announced, "This is the first book I ever read by myself." As the class becomes more familiar with LSCs and students become more fluent readers, longer, more complex books can be successfully introduced.

Does the Teacher Know the Book?

We both know how important it is to have read and enjoyed the books that we offer for LSCs. Without this firsthand knowledge, it is next to impossible to do an enthusiastic or convincing booktalk. It also affects the group discussion. We can both remember occasions when we did not follow our own advice. For example, Katharine once had several copies of Paula Fox's *Maurice's Room* and decided to offer it as one of the LSC choices. She had enjoyed reading other books by Fox and assumed that she would enjoy this one. Time ran out and she did not read *Maurice's Room* before the booktalk deadline. Once she did read it, she found it to be disjointed and lacking in compelling characters. In short, Katharine disliked the book and as a result found it hard to be a part of the LSC because she really wanted to point out all the book's limitations. She knew better than to do this, however, as she did not want to undermine the students, who had enjoyed the book's humor and exaggerations. Katharine was a listener rather than an active participant. The discussion among the students was successful, but Katharine's role in the group was not very satisfying.

Some teachers have asked us, "But why should it matter if you like the book?" We have found that if we are to have any role in the group other than as a listener, we need to feel a connection with the book.

Fortunately, although our goal is not to have students like the same books we do, we have rarely selected a book that most of the group did not enjoy. On occasion, one or two students have not enjoyed a certain book, and this has led to some extremely rich discussions. Once in a while, all of the students have come to the first group discussion agreeing that the book was boring. However, in the process of discussing how boring the book was, students have often come to view the book in a different light. For example, when evaluating LSCs, Barbara commented on how she changed her mind about Sid Fleischman's *The Whipping Boy:*

> When I read a book called *Whipping Boy* I did not like it but when we got in our literature circle I learned that I did like the book but I just did not understand it.

As students have many opportunities throughout the week to read books that they have chosen for themselves, we approach LSCs as an opportunity to introduce students to authors and books they may not come across otherwise. For example, many of the girls in Gail's class love to read the Babysitters Club series of books. While Gail is delighted that they are enthusiastically reading these books, she prefers to use more richly developed texts for LSCs. She does not make judgements in front of the students, however, as this would undermine her goal of enhancing their reading development and experiences.

Does the Book Relate to Other Topics of Study?

Gail tries to offer LSC books that relate to issues and topics being studied by the class. For example, when the class was investigating immigration, she decided to offer five books that address the experiences of children whose families emigrated from another country to the United States. *The Star Fisher* by Laurence Yep explores the experiences of a Chinese immigrant family that settles in the South in an all-white neighborhood. *Children of the River,* as described earlier, is about a Cambodian teenager who flees from her homeland and settles in Oregon. In *Lupita Mañana* by Patricia Beatty, two teenage Mexican siblings cross the border without papers looking for their "rich" aunt who lives in Indio, California. *America Street,* edited by Anne Mazer, is a collection of short stories by authors of color, and *The Hundred Dresses* by Eleanor Estes is about a Polish girl whose family settles in New York at the turn of the century.

Sometimes we cannot find many books on a topic being investigated by the class; perhaps only one or two titles can be found. For example, when the class went on a field trip to hear the San Francisco Symphony

Orchestra, they had lunch in a park outside City Hall. A homeless man approached the children and asked if he could have any lunch that they didn't eat. This single encounter really affected the children, prompting the class to embark on a study of the homeless. As part of this study, Gail located two books that addressed the issue and offered them as LSC choices. *The Family Under the Bridge* by Natalie Carlson is a short novel about a homeless man living under the arches of the bridges of the Seine River in Paris, France. The second book, *Monkey Island* by Paula Fox, is a longer novel about a young boy who is abandoned by his mother and ends up living in the streets with two homeless men.

Locating the Books

We find that we need about ten copies of each title. In this way, groups are kept small enough to be manageable (no more than eight students per group), there is a copy for the teacher, and there are one or two extra copies for occasions when students forget to bring their books to school. Teachers ask, "But where do you get these books?" We have written small grants. We have collected copies of a book from different libraries; sometimes, students have helped to locate the copies or have brought in their own. We have raided the school's book room, where class sets of books are stored. We have borrowed books from other teachers. We have used bonus points from book clubs to buy sets (though we don't rely on the book clubs, as they tend not to have many multicultural books or books written by authors of color). We take a good look at the trade books included in the district-adopted literature-based reading series. We have used carefully-selected stories in reading texts, but only those that are unexcerpted and unabridged. We have bought books in garage sales and secondhand bookstores. (This will not usually generate a set of books, but it can help replace lost books or add to an emerging set.) A friend of ours, Barbara Schmidt, sends a letter home to parents with book club orders (see Figure 2). In the letter, she makes suggestions for parents about books and authors. She also invites families to buy books for LSCs, indicating these titles with a star (see Figure 3). Donations are acknowledged with a bookplate attached to the inside front cover of the book, indicating the donor and the date of the donation ("This book was donated by

Dear Parents:

Attached is the latest order form from the Trumpet Book Club and the Scholastic Book Club. There are many wonderful books that I am certain your child will enjoy, and these books are considered "good" literature. Therefore I am attaching a suggested list of books to order.

There are also a few titles I would like to order for our Reader's Workshop (literature) program, and I have put a star next to these titles. If you would like to purchase/donate one or more of these books please fill out the tear-off on the bottom of the Suggested Book List that I have attached and send it in with your child's book order. Also, include the donated book title on your child's order form. Your child's name will be noted in the book as the person who donated it to Room 13.

Thank you for your help in adding to our literature library. It has been through the kindness and generosity of the parents in Room 13 that we have developed an exciting selection of books. Your addition will be extremely appreciated.

I would like to thank those children whose parents donated books to our class from the last order: Becky C., Derek S., Seth C-G., and Dariana S.

Sincerely,

Barbara Schmidt

Figure 2 A teacher's letter to parents about a book club order

C. J. Smith's family in April 1994"). In this way, Barbara has been able to build up her LSC library. Gail has asked her students to purchase a particular book from a book club order. Other teachers have requested funds from the PTA. As more schools move toward literature-based reading programs, money formerly used for textbooks is being used to purchase sets of trade books instead. In cases where many teachers in a school are implementing LSCs, a centrally located book room seems to work

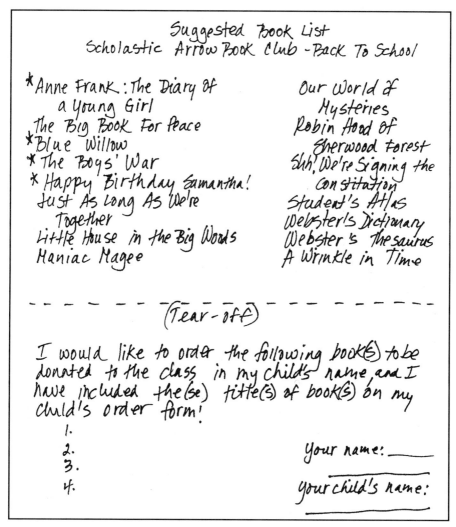

Suggested Book List
Scholastic Arrow Book Club - Back To School

*Anne Frank: The Diary of
    a Young Girl
,The Big Book For Peace
*Blue Willow
* The Boys' War
* Happy Birthday Samantha!
Just As Long As We're
    Together
Little House in the Big Woods
Maniac Magee

Our World of
    Mysteries
Robin Hood of
    Sherwood Forest
Shh! We're Signing the
    Constitution
Student's Atlas
Webster's Dictionary
Webster's Thesaurus
A Wrinkle in Time

- - - - - - - (Tear-off) - - - - - - - -

I would like to order the following book(s) to be
donated to the class in my child's name, and I
have included the(se) title(s) of book(s) on my
child's order form!
    1.
    2.
    3.
    4.

Your name: _____

your child's name: _____

Figure 3 A teacher's suggested list of books to be purchased

out well—in this way, teachers pool their resources, thereby reducing the financial burden for each.

Offering Book Choices to Students

Giving students choice goes a long way toward motivating them to read. For most of their school lives, they have been told what to read. We have seen how elated students can be when they get their first choice and how quickly they rush to their seats and start reading in spite of the activity going on around them.

In reality, their choice in LSCs is limited to four or five books. Even this limited choice can have a profound impact on how invested students are in their reading. Many of them become experienced and fluent readers and go on to select from a much wider selection of books. In the case of students who continue to struggle, their reading choices may be limited to the LSC selections. They often take longer to read a book, often find it difficult to read for sustained periods of time, and if they are reading aloud with a partner, it is inevitable that it will take them longer to finish a book. Consequently, not much time may be left over for independent reading. One learning event that seems to encourage these students' development as independent readers is their involvement in a cross-age reading program, such as the one that Gail and Mary Pippitt, a first/second grade teacher, began several years ago (see Samway, Whang, and Pippitt 1995). In preparation for working with younger children, all the older students have to read and select from a wide selection of shorter books. (We address the issue of the needs of less fluent readers more fully in Chapter 5.)

In most cases, a book is offered more than once. Gail usually rotates a selection of four books each month, from which students ultimately read three. When Katharine has led LSCs, she has varied the selections more frequently, as the following list illustrates:

- Week 1:
  Sadako and the Thousand Paper Cranes
  The Hundred-Penny Box
  JT
  All It Takes Is Practice

- Week 2:
  The Hundred-Penny Box
  All It Takes Is Practice
  Matilda
  Circle of Gold

- Week 3:
  Circle of Gold
  Matilda
  JT
  In the Year of the Boar and Jackie Robinson

- Week 4:
  In the Year of the Boar and Jackie Robinson
  The War with Grandpa
  The Gift-Giver
  The Hundred Dresses

- Week 5:
  The Hundred Dresses
  The War with Grandpa
  The Cat Ate My Gymsuit
  Charlie Pippin

- Week 6:
  Charlie Pippin
  The Cat Ate My Gymsuit
  The Gift-Giver
  Fantastic Mr. Fox

As this list illustrates, most books are offered at least twice during a six-week period. The decision of whether to offer a book a second or subsequent time depends entirely on the interest of the students. This list also shows how the books offered in the first weeks are shorter and can be read more quickly so that students are more likely to have a successful first experience. Throughout the year shorter, less complex books are made available so that less fluent readers can fully participate in LSCs.

Establishing a Supportive Classroom Community

A recent theme in educational circles is the need to teach social skills (for example, working cooperatively and listening attentively and respectfully to others) in addition to cognitive skills. For several years, Gail has focused on social skills throughout the day. In addition to cooperative learning activities, her students are part of a community-building experience, *Tribes* (Gibbs 1994), which will be discussed in greater detail in Chapter 4. Through daily class meetings, direct teaching of social skills, debriefing sessions in which students reflect on what they have learned, and expressions of appreciation for what others have done to support them, Gail and her students have created a supportive classroom environment. Students learn that it is OK to share concerns, worries, and fears with their peers.

LSCs have gone a long way toward building this sense of community in the classroom. Through the open-ended discussions, students often get to know each other more intimately than they might otherwise. A spirit of trust emerges. If a classroom is contentious and class members—students and teachers—do not treat others respectfully, it will be hard to have successful LSCs, because honest, insightful discussions require that participants feel safe with each other. Classrooms that have used LSCs successfully have certain features in common: meaningful learning activities, an absence of put-downs, an appreciation of differences, and teachers who listen to and observe their students very carefully so as to inform their teaching.

We were surprised to discover that at first some students have a hard time disagreeing with each other in LSCs because they think that disagreement will be construed as a put-down. They confuse put-downs with respectful disagreement. Whenever Gail notices this, she makes sure to address the issue in a minilesson. On one occasion, the discussion evolved in the following way:

GAIL: During this discussion, will we all have the same ideas?
DAMLONGSONG: No, we have different opinion.
GAIL: Can you disagree with your friends? Does it mean that you are angry with your friend if you disagree with him or her?
(*Some students seem a bit hesitant.*)
LANCE: No, we all have different ideas and it's OK.
GAIL: It's great to have different ideas. That's how we're going to learn about and appreciate the book in new ways. So why don't we get

started. You don't have to raise your hand to speak. We'll do it pop-corn style, speak whenever you want, but one at a time.

Gail tried to prepare students for the fact that in a discussion they would not necessarily agree with each other, and that disagreement would not necessarily imply anger. She also reminded them that in a real discussion people don't raise their hands and wait to be called on; they just speak.

Establishing Routines

If a class is to run smoothly, routines must be established. This is particularly true for LSCs, as students spend quite a bit of time working independently. In this section we address the routines we have found to be important in the successful implementation of LSCs.

Students Selecting Books

When Gail gives a booktalk, she describes each book and then invites students to decide which books they will read. If too many want the same title, she uses a lottery system to decide who gets the book. Titles are available on more than one occasion, so if students do not get to read their first choice right away, it is likely to be available in a later LSC. LSC titles are also always available for independent reading.

Once the books have been distributed, students meet in groups to decide how long they will need to finish the book. They also negotiate with Gail a deadline for when the book must be completed. Gail already has an idea of how long the book will take to complete, but she takes into consideration the students' suggestions, as well as events scheduled for the coming week, such as assemblies and field trips. Once the group has agreed on a date, the names of the group members and the due date are recorded on a sheet of paper, which is posted on the wall so everyone can see it. At the beginning of the year, when students are reading shorter selections—for example, *JT* (Wagner), *The Friendship* and *The Gold Cadillac* (M. Taylor), *Song of the Trees* (M. Taylor), or *A Taste of Blackberries* (D. B. Smith)—they have three or four days to complete a book.

Toward the middle of the year, when books are often longer, they have from seven to ten days. As a group does not usually meet until the book is finished, it is important that all the students understand how much they must read each day, either in class or at home, in order to be prepared for the initial discussion. If a book is more complex or is hard to get into, Gail meets briefly with students to help them get launched into the book. Some teachers we know use written contracts in which students identify how much they must read each day. Gail has not found this necessary for the whole class, but uses contracts with individual students who are having a hard time completing books on time.

The degree to which reading is a social act is reflected in the fact that some students quickly discuss the available LSC books with their friends and then make a joint decision. Sometimes these decisions lead to a particularly enjoyable literary experience. At other times, pairing enables a less fluent reader to understand and enjoy a book.

Time to Read

When Gail first introduced her class to LSCs, she noticed that the students were thrilled about having time in class to read. In the past, Gail, like many other teachers, hadn't allocated much time for real reading. Her classes had spent lots of time learning about reading, but not much time actually reading. She now realizes that if she wants students to become successful readers who enjoy what they are reading, they need time during the school day to read. Gail remembers hearing a statistic that the average time students read in class is less than five minutes a day. Her students now have considerably more than five minutes a day for reading.

Once LSC books have been chosen, the reading begins. At the beginning of the year, the students can usually read for only about fifteen minutes before getting restless. As they become more accustomed to the routine of reading independently, the time they can spend reading becomes longer and longer. By the end of the year, most students can read comfortably for an hour. By providing time in class for everyone to read, including the teacher, a community of readers begins to form. Students reading the same book often change seats to be close to each other so they can quietly chat about what they are reading. The quiet calmness that now characterizes the room provides a supportive environment for students to read, think, and write in their literature logs. There is a relationship between having time in school to read, selecting one's own books, and becoming hooked on books.

Preparing for the Discussion

When Gail was new to LSCs, she sometimes wondered whether students were reading the whole book. There were times when students would come to a discussion circle, say something that was very similar to what she had said when introducing the book to the class (for example, "This book, *Tuck Everlasting*, is about living forever"), and then contribute very little else to the discussion. We have found it helpful to check in with students before a discussion begins to make sure they have finished reading the book. In order to have a rich discussion, all members of the group need to have read the book. It is true that one can learn a lot from listening, but we believe that each group member has a responsibility to come prepared. If a student has not completed the LSC book in time for the first discussion, he or she does not participate in the discussion. When they finish the book, they join the group for the follow-up discussion. By and large, once students have experienced LSCs, most find the discussions so stimulating that they finish the books in time.

Sometimes students have a hard time getting into a book and say it is boring. In such a case, Gail encourages them to read on, often sharing an interesting detail from the book. For example, *Tuck Everlasting* (Babbitt) is a favorite book, but many students have difficulty getting into it, mainly because the first fifty pages set the scene. One day, during independent reading time, Gail noticed that several students who were reading *Tuck Everlasting* were fidgeting in their seats, looking around the room, and beginning to talk with their neighbors. When she asked them to continue reading, some students said that the book was boring and that they didn't understand what was happening in the story. It was at this point that Gail offered assistance. She called the group together, read the book aloud to them, and helped them get involved. Similarly, some students who were reading *Black Star, Bright Dawn* (O'Dell) had difficulty understanding the beginning of the book, which starts with a seal hunt, an important part of the Eskimo culture, but one with which students were unfamiliar. Again, Gail had a short meeting with the group, explained what was happening, and answered questions.

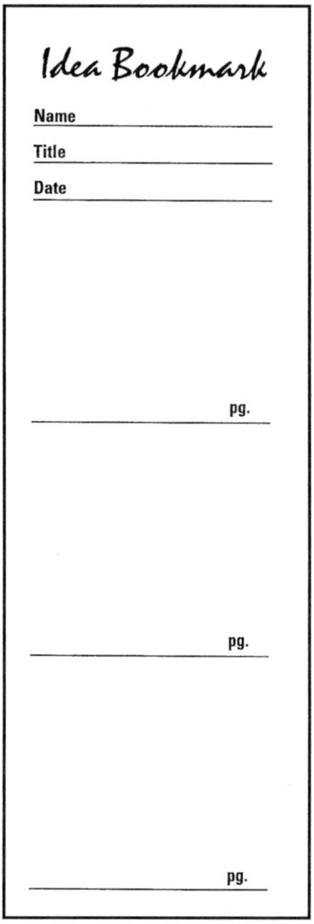

Figure 4 An idea bookmark

This brief meeting helped the students get over their initial hurdle, and they ended up enjoying the book.

We encourage students to record their ongoing responses to a book while reading it. Each student picks up one or more idea bookmarks (Figure 4) when beginning to read a new book. These bookmarks have sections in which students jot down notes in preparation for the upcoming LSC. They often comment on parts they found particularly enjoyable, questions they have, and sections that evoked a strong emotional response. They also include page numbers for quick reference. For example, while reading *America Street* (Mazer), Esmeralda wrote the following comments on idea bookmarks: "It was stupid of that girl to

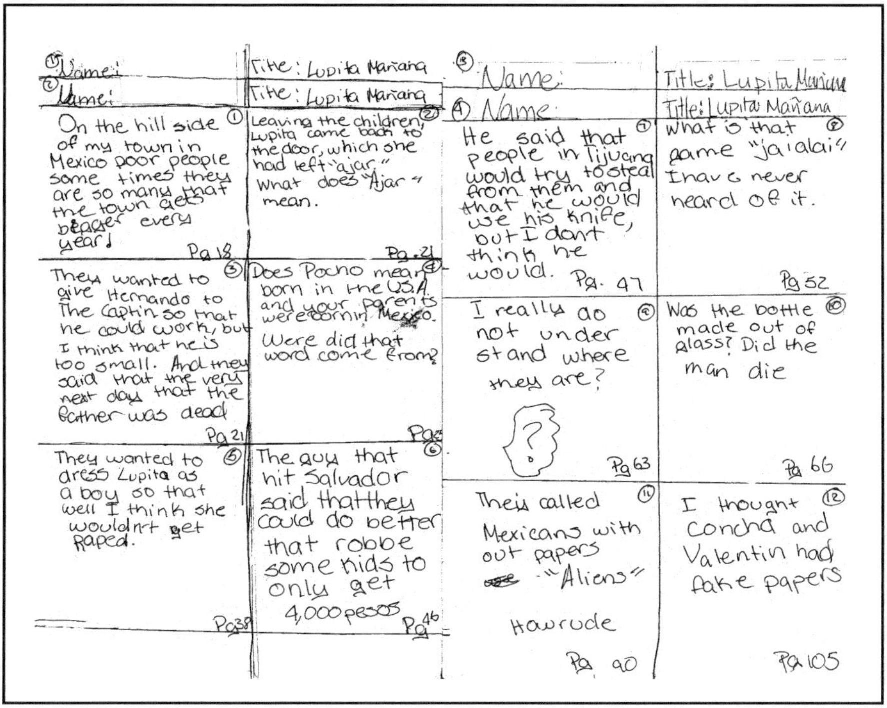

Figure 5 Angelina's double-entry idea bookmarks

get in the wrong lunch line because she knew she could of gotten in trouble. Pg. 33" and "I thought it was scary for the boy when he went into a coma because he could of never awoken from it. Pg. 8." When she came to the first discussion she brought with her several idea bookmarks and regularly referred to them during the discussion, as if to jog her memory. Sometimes she read directly from them. In contrast, Angelina rarely read from her idea bookmarks, even though she was a prolific writer of them. In fact, she designed her own double-entry bookmark (see Figure 5). She appeared to find them invaluable while reading.

When they finish a book, students reflect on it in their literature logs. Entries written after students have finished reading a book serve several purposes. In the long term, they provide students with a detailed record of what they have read and their responses to books over a year, which is useful information for both the students and Gail to have when assessing

---

LITERATURE JOURNALS

Each time you write in your journal:

Write the date.
Write the title of the book.
Write the author's name.
Do not skip lines.

In this journal, you, your friends, and I will be talking about BOOKS, AUTHORS, READING, and WRITING. It will be like writing letters to each other. In these letters, I ask that you TELL US ABOUT THE BOOKS YOU ARE READING:

- tell us what you noticed
- tell us what you thought
- tell us what you felt
- tell us what you were reminded of
- tell us what you liked and what you didn't like and why
- tell us what lesson you learned from the story
- ask questions or ask for help

Write in your journal at least TWO TIMES A WEEK. I will read and respond to it once every two weeks at least.

Figure 6 Gail's guidelines for literature logs

student progress. In the short term, they help students prepare for discussions. Eata demonstrated their usefulness when assessing the LSC program at the end of the year. He referred to the literature log as being like "a brain with pages . . . [that] help me remember what book I read and what happen in the book."

Gail provides written guidelines for the literature logs, which are stapled on the inside front cover of the logs (see Figure 6). She sometimes notices that students use the list of suggested topics as a mandate and respond superficially to every topic in the guidelines. This observation is a clue to her that she needs to spend time teaching the students that the list presents options, that they can choose what they respond to, and that their choice should be based on the particular book and their response to it.

Entries often reflect on the plot and characters. Students also make connections between books and their own lives, as the following entry written by Malcolm after reading *The Kid in the Red Jacket* (Park) illustrates:

> I like this book cause it tells me alot if you move from a state to another you would feel like you don't know anybody. This once happened to me when I just came to this school. It was like nobody know me. When I was going to my new school I was very excited. Then when I went there I was trying to make friend with this kid. Then he told me to get my face out of here. Then I told him that I was just making friend with him.

In past years, Gail asked students to write frequently in their logs, but after introducing idea bookmarks, students commented that multiple literature log entries on the same book seemed redundant. They now write in their logs only when they have finished a book.

The idea bookmarks and the literature logs serve two distinct functions. Whereas the idea bookmarks are useful for spontaneous, sometimes random thoughts, the literature logs provide students with an opportunity to reflect in greater detail on a book. Students are encouraged to write short comments and questions on the idea bookmarks and more in-depth reflections in their literature logs. On one occasion, when reading *All It Takes Is Practice* (Miles), Sylvia wrote twenty-three entries on four bookmarks. Her entries included the following: "I really liked Peter because he really whanted to play with Stuart and sometimes black parents tell the son or daughters to dont play with white people but she didn't say that." Her final idea bookmark entry was, "I wouldn't reccomend this book to someone who loves description. this book doesn't have description." After she had finished the book, Sylvia wrote the following entry in her literature log:

> Well I think that this book is good book but does not have really description but what I really like is while I am reading I am always waiting for something else to happend like when Stuart and Peter

got jumped by those two kids I really was exited I was waiting for more it really gets me hooked. I think that the boys friend the one that loves playing basketball but can't because she's a girl that's dumb any kid even if she is a girl could play a sport and I though that was not fair for the girl. the rest was okey but like I said they should of put description in it so it could be more interesting.

Open-ended Discussions About Books

A key characteristic of LSCs is that discussions are open-ended. Instead of engineering a discussion, teachers follow the lead of students. In contrast, in many elementary classrooms, teachers ask questions and students answer them. Discourse patterns reveal that the teacher is the most frequent speaker, the most frequent asker of questions, the all-knowing source of information. In these classrooms, students rarely interact with each other if the teacher is a member of the group. Discussion in this type of classroom has been called a "gentle inquisition." But in LSCs the discussion more closely resembles a "grand conversation" (Edelsky 1988; Eeds and Wells 1989). Group members question each other, and they agree and disagree with each other. The teacher is, to a large extent, just one more member of the group, albeit an experienced, knowledgeable reader. When teachers lead LSCs, they are not interested in students voicing the teachers' understanding of and views on the book; instead, they are interested in hearing how a book moved students; connections students make between the book, other books, and their life experiences; and students' interpretations of and views on the book. It is particularly exciting when students express different points of view, as this often leads to some fascinating and substantive conversations.

When students are new to LSCs, they aren't sure what to expect or what to do; as a result, they tend to be quiet. Many students are not accustomed to having a discussion in a group in which the teacher is a co-participant. Facilitators of LSCs need to be patient and understand that for many students it takes time to learn and understand this new role of being an active participant with the teacher. One strategy that helps is to consistently open the discussion with an open-ended question—"So, what do you think of this book?" or "What did this book make you think of?"—and then wait for someone in the group to speak up. Occasionally, a second open-ended question has to be asked, almost as an assurance to the students that the teacher is really interested in their insights and opinions. If students are to take ownership of the discussions, they have to be given opportunities to raise issues that interest or concern them, right from the beginning of the discussion. As students become more familiar with the structure of LSCs, they generally don't need even an opening question. In fact, when learner-centered, open-ended discussions are respected and encouraged, discussions are likely to begin even before the teacher joins the group.

Many teachers who are accustomed to orchestrating discussions from a comprehension standpoint ("Who are the main characters?" "What happened next?" "Let's talk about . . .") may find it difficult to let go and follow the natural flow of the conversation. Also, it is often difficult for teachers to wait in silence while students pull their thoughts together. It may be even harder for them to take this less dominant role if they have not had many opportunities to talk about books with their own friends and colleagues and experience the energy that is created when one is allowed to express (and back up) one's reactions and opinions. Even when one has had opportunities to engage in LSCs as adults, it can still be hard to hold back and let a conversation evolve without heavy-handed guidance. When Katharine first led an LSC, a friend with whom she was team teaching pointed out that Katharine was not giving students time to think. She would ask an open-ended question and when there was no immediate response from one of the group members, she would either ask another question or make a comment in order to fill the void. Until her friend told her this, Katharine hadn't realized how uncomfortable she had been with silence. Since then, she has been able to accommodate much longer periods of silence, and has learned that if she remains quiet, someone else will usually speak and this encourages other students to speak up.

When we ask students to evaluate LSCs, the overwhelming response is how much they enjoy and look forward to the discussions. When comparing her former experiences with book discussions in school and LSCs, Amphaivane commented that she preferred LSCs because "We share our thoughts and feelings of the book and we don't have to wait till it's our turn—we do it popcorn style." Sylvia remarked on how she thought that speaking up in the discussions had led to an improvement in her reading:

> Well I have improved in my reading alot because I youse to never pay attention to the book all I did was read and read without knowing what the book was about. I have improved because now I talk alot in the conversation and I take alot of notes about the book alot of examples and I youse to never share. I youse to be very shy and I always thought that what I was going to say was wrong but I have realize that everyone has difrent opinions and it doesn't mean they are wrong. Now I believe in myself and I share as much as I want to.

Students frequently comment on how, in previous years, the book discussions involved formal turn-taking, which they were not very fond of. Amphaivane pointed out how LSC discussions are more spontaneous and more satisfying:

> What I think about this year's literature program is better than last year I guess because this year's literature program is kind of more better in life. Last year we went around the circle but this year's literature program is like well you just say it right away not just wait till it was your turn you just say it right away.

Other students also enjoyed the less structured format of the discussions and the way in which they were free to share their opinions and reactions. Mano was particularly appreciative of the way in which the open-ended discussions allowed for honest and thoughtful dialogue. She wrote, "My fav. thing about the discussions are the honesty, and the different opinions we all have."

It is important to teach students how to be successful conversationalists, especially at the beginning of the year when they are new to LSCs. This is particularly true when students enter the class without having had many opportunities for open-ended discussions. Gail uses a minilesson format to introduce students to critical elements inherent in a good conversation: responding to each other, not just the teacher; building on previous comments; sharing similar ideas; jumping into a conversation;

disagreeing respectfully; asking questions; and being prepared to offer evidence to support a point of view. Gail gives these minilessons when she sees a need for them—when she notices that students are confused about their role in a discussion; when students constantly look to the teacher for comments, approval, and direction; when students are reluctant to disagree with each other or chide each other for having a different opinion; or when students engage in parallel talk instead of interacting with each other's ideas. One day, during the debriefing session that followed a discussion on *The Friendship* (M. Taylor), Lance commented that he hadn't talked. It turned out that he hadn't kept any notes in his literature log and had a hard time remembering the story, which he had finished reading several days earlier. This prompted Gail to give a minilesson on ways to prepare for a discussion. She began by asking students who spoke up in LSCs to reflect on the strategies they used to prepare themselves for the discussion:

GAIL: Those of you that are speaking up in the discussion and responding, what are you doing to prepare for this discussion? So that some of the others can learn from you.

AROMRACK: Take notes.

GAIL: So you thought about it ahead of time? OK. What about the rest of you? What do you do to prepare for the discussion?

NAM: When, when I heard some ideas, I just commented on them.

EMERY: (*inaudible*) bring our own ideas.

GAIL: OK, and what else are you doing in the group?

AROMRACK: Commenting. Some people bring a different idea, and then I bring up another (*inaudible*).

GAIL: Uh-huh. So it sounds like you're listening to what other people are saying. So there's a lot of listening going on. OK, what else do you do?

NAM: Just pay attention to what happens in the book.

While we want all students to contribute to discussions so that we can all learn together, we also understand that people have different personalities and styles of interaction. There have been times when we have inadvertently put pressure on students to speak up. This has come to our attention through the written reflections of particularly shy students such as Choulaphone, who commented that she liked it when people took turns talking and nobody laughed when she was speaking; however, she also remarked on how pressured she sometimes felt to speak:

> I don't really like to be presure to talk when I'am in the discussion group. Because when I try to say something nothing is going to come out. And some time I get embarass. I just want to talk without any body telling me that is my turn. I just want to talk when somebody is finishing talking.

Lynn demonstrated considerable compassion for her peers who are less verbal when she offered a strategy for including them in the discussion. She wrote:

> I think the group don't share that much because sometimes they might feel left out, sometimes I feel left out also. What we could do to get them to share is to tell them that we are really concerned about what they have to say and make them feel like their's [they're] part of the group.

It can be a delicate balancing act to encourage students to share their responses while respecting their need to be quiet. However, if there is a trusting classroom climate, even the quietest students are likely to speak up.

Arriving at an Assignment

During the group discussion, it helps to take notes (see Figure 7). Having to concentrate on recording the content of a discussion is one way for teachers to keep the focus away from them during the discussion. This is particularly important when students are new to LSCs. The notes also help in the formulation of follow-up assignments. When the discussion is nearing an end, it's a good idea to summarize the discussion, as Gail did toward the end of a first discussion of *Scorpions* (Myers):

GAIL: OK. It sounds like you all really liked the book and we talked about things where you got hooked, parts that you really liked. Some of the ideas that came out were, Eata was talking about how he thought this

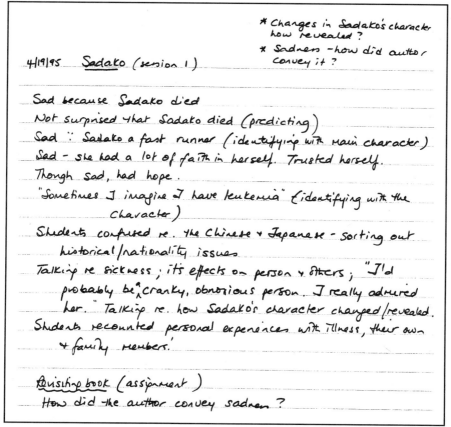

Figure 7 *Notes on a discussion*

book was about friendship between Tito and Jamal and what that friendship means. And then Kadedra talked about the relationship between Mr. Davidson and Jamal. It sounds like you really got angry when you were reading about the way he screamed at Jamal. And we talked about gangs, what it is to be a part of a gang. And then we talked about the fight and about where we got hooked.

Once the discussion is summarized, a follow-up assignment can be made. Often, while we're keeping notes during the discussion, we jot down possible ideas for assignments. The notes in the top right-hand corner of Figure 7 indicate two ideas that occurred to Katharine during one LSC; both

Book Title Star fisher

LITERATURE STUDY CIRCLES

Name: Patrick Date: 6/23/94 Session: 1	Prepared for Discussion +	Participated in the Discussion +	Notes: Great-great grandmothers came from Ireland and Russia. (Making connections to own life and history)
Name: Esmeralda	Prepared for Discussion +	Participated in the Discussion +	Notes: Don't judge a person from outside. (theme?, prejudice?)
Name: Kim Lon	Prepared for Discussion +	Participated in the Discussion +	Notes: One boy said to me & friends once "you should be going back to your country if you don't all know English." (personal connections, discrimination/prejudice)
Name: Sylvia	Prepared for Discussion +	Participated in the Discussion +	Notes: It's really hard to be 2 persons — speak Spanish —home English - School (living in 2 worlds, cross-cultural experience)
Name: Lance	Prepared for Discussion +	Participated in the Discussion ✓	Notes: When you don't talk another lang. it's hard to understand. Might think you're stupid (Difficulties exper. by immigrants)
Name: Tamara	Prepared for Discussion +	Participated in the Discussion +	Notes: Lots of people think all Americans have blond hair / blue eyes - (Who is an American?)
Name:	Prepared for Discussion	Participated in the Discussion	Notes: Assignment: What do you think the theme of the book is? ... evidence

Figure 8 Gail's notes on a discussion

arose out of the discussion, and the final assignment (at the bottom of the page) was grounded in one of the ideas. Figure 8 is an example of the type of note-taking that Gail finds most helpful. Listing each participant's name and jotting down comments made during the discussion on this form help Gail summarize the discussion and arrive at an assignment.

Teachers ask us whether students decide on their own assignments. Sometimes students initiate an assignment, and this can be thrilling. We believe, however, that teachers must play a prominent role in this decision, drawing upon their knowledge of literature and writing to stretch students. After all, one of the purposes of the second and any subsequent sessions is to begin to look more closely at the craft of writing and literary elements.

Asking students to revisit a book through the assignment serves several purposes. It prepares them for a subsequent discussion that is often more focused and in-depth than the first. It is also a means to explore what authors do so as to make younger writers more aware of the craft of writing and to give them access to additional writing techniques. It is very important to build on the excitement that is generated in the discussion when deciding on the assignment.

In general, assignments fall in two categories: those that continue to explore issues the book raises, and those that focus on literary elements. The following lists illustrate the kinds of assignments that have evolved out of discussions we have had with students:

Assignments that continue to explore issues

Jar of Dreams (Uchida):

Find examples of stereotypes and racism in the book.

Go back and look at where Rinko changed. Why did she change?

The Star Fisher (Yep):

Find examples where Joan changed and started to appreciate her family more.

The Friendship (M. Taylor):

Go back to the story and think about Mr. Tom Bee. What kind of person was he? Find places in the book that illustrate this.

The Cat Ate My Gymsuit (Danziger):

Think about freedom of speech. Do you think you have the right to say what you want, no matter what?

Children of the River (Crew):

This book made you think of the Blue Lagoon. In what ways?

Assignments that explore literary elements

The Cay (T. Taylor):

How did the author reveal changes in the young boy's character?

The Friendship (M. Taylor):

What kind of person is Tom Bee? Find evidence for how Mildred Taylor portrays Tom Bee.

The Gold Cadillac (M. Taylor):

How does Mildred Taylor show racism in this story?

Tuck Everlasting (Babbitt):

Find places where you got hooked in the story. What did the author do to hook you?

Matilda (Dahl):
How does Roald Dahl make his audience laugh?
Scorpions (Myers):
What does the author do to make you feel like you're there in the book?
Song of the Trees (M. Taylor):
What do you think is the theme of the book? Find evidence to back up your answer.
Children of the River (Crew):
Find examples of how the character is caught between two cultures. How does the author convey the conflict?
Figure out how Linda Crew managed to make you feel that you were right there in the book. How did she make it seem so real?
Iggie's House (Blume):
What do you think the theme of the book is? Provide evidence to back up your opinion.
Scorpions (Myers):
What are some things that Walter Dean Myers does as a writer in the fight scene to make it so real and vivid?
The Hundred Dresses (Estes):
Find out how the author reveals meanness in the characters.
Sadako and the Thousand Paper Cranes (Coerr):
How does the author manage to convey such sadness in this book?

It is important that the follow-up assignment be grounded in the discussion. This is not to say that we do not come to a discussion with an idea in mind about a possible assignment. This is one way in which we prepare ourselves for the discussion. However, during the course of the discussion, our initial ideas frequently change. For example, when Gail read *Children of the River,* she was moved by the conflict that Sundara faced in confronting two very different cultures. When she met with her students, though, the discussion touched on quite different issues—teenage relationships, fleeing Cambodia, family pressures, different customs, and the particularly poignant moments that captivated the students. It was clear to Gail that if she had given the assignment that she had in mind before the discussion started, she would have been negating the rich dialogue that had occurred. In synthesizing this particular discussion, she understood that a dominant issue had been that all of the students had been moved by the book and thoroughly engaged as readers. Instead of asking the group to look at the cross-cultural conflict that most struck Gail, however, she asked the students to find places in the book where Linda Crew had hooked them as readers, and to figure out how Crew managed to do this.

Later in the year, another group of students read the same book. In this case, the issue of being a member of two cultures, a home culture and a school culture, was a dynamic part of the discussion. Gail therefore suggested that everyone explore the conflict that Sundara faced when living in two cultures. Sylvia prepared for the second discussion by reflecting on the topic in her literature log:

> One thing that got me hooked on the book was that how good Linda Crew described how hard it was going to be for Soundara to be both cultures American and also Cambodian at the same time. I though that was very difficult because at home her aunty will tell her to be a Cambodian you have to do what Cambodians do and when she went to school Jonathan will tell her that she was in America that she had to act like American. I don't think I would be able to handle that.

Gail used to assign a lot of projects and activities that were grounded in the books that the children were reading, but that did not really encourage students to explore the books in greater detail, and did not deepen their understanding of the book. For example, students would be asked to write a sequel to the book, write another chapter, make posters and dioramas, and write book reports. We generally do not recommend such assignments, as we prefer that students use the available time to actually read and discuss books. It is true that students sometimes enjoy responding to books in ways that do not rely exclusively on oral or written language. Students should have opportunities to respond to literature in as many different ways as possible, but follow-up activities or assignments should be authentic and should extend their language and literacy. (Chapter 5 addresses this issue in greater detail.)

When first introducing students to LSCs, teacher and students should work on an assignment together, so that students can familiarize themselves with what is often a very new learning experience. Later on, they can work either independently or together. Students (and the teacher) have one or two days in which to complete the assignment. Some students use class time to complete their assignments, and often begin right after the discussion. Other students take the assignment home. Assignments do not require that students reread the book. Instead, they usually involve the students' browsing through the book, seeking out passages that relate to the assignment. It helps if the book is fresh in the reader's mind.

Follow-up Sessions

The first session is often devoted to personal, aesthetic responses to the literature. As we mentioned previously, second sessions sometimes involve a similar exploration of the book, albeit with a greater focus than is usually found in initial session. Often, though, the second and sometimes subsequent sessions focus more on an analysis of literary elements, such as plot development, how an author reveals a character, or the role of the narrator.

In a discussion about *The Friendship* (M. Taylor), the group was talking about Mr. Tom Bee's character. Paul commented, "I think, [he's] brave. He went back to the store to get, um, to get some tobacco and when he saw the white men all around, he stood up and called Mr. John Wallace by his first name." This was just one of many comments that students made to illustrate how courageous they thought Tom Bee was. The discussion revolved around character traits and plot elements; the two are intertwined in this book.

It isn't always easy for students to go from responding affectively to looking more analytically at how the author achieved the effects that they notice and comment on. Students find it helpful to mark the pages in the book where they find evidence to support their viewpoint. Post-its or idea bookmarks inserted into the book also help the students make these literary connections. LSC book discussions are very effective, natural ways in which to extend students' knowledge of writing and books. Instead of teaching about literary elements in a decontextualized fashion (for example, isolated lessons with follow-up exercises on plot, theme, descriptive writing, or point of view), it makes much more sense to explore these issues and introduce students to the related terminology in a context where they are engaged, excited, and motivated. We encourage students to constantly make connections between their responses to the book, the author's craft, and what they can do themselves as writers. We teach students how to prepare for second discussions, particularly when they are new to LSCs. Even later in the year, it may be necessary to return to the same issues, as the following example illustrates. The students had begun talking about where the author had hooked them. Gail asked them if they could direct group members to particular pages so they could look more closely at the text:

GAIL: And let's look at her writing and see what it was about the way she wrote it that hooked you.

ANGELINA: The part that she said that her heart was something.

GAIL: OK. That's what I'm saying.

ANGELINA: Oh.

GAIL: Do you know what page it was on? See, when you *do* get hooked, it's good to put the page down so we can actually look at the writing and see how authors hook us.

Angelina found a part in the book that illustrated her point and read a short section. Gail asked her what it was about that section that hooked her and Angelina responded, "There's a lot of description and action." This led to the group discussing ways in which the author used descriptive language in such a way that they felt that they could visualize the setting:

GAIL: Description, too? Like what?

MARÍA: Oh, like when they put the wooden bed, or whatever—

SYLVIA (*interrupting*): Instead of saying, "Bed."

ANGELINA: Yeah.

GAIL: OK. So they describe the bed. You're picturing it more. How about this one here? (*Reading from the book.*) "Hot fear burned her chest."

SYLVIA: Oh. How she was, um,

ANGELINA: Worried.

SYLVIA: Yeah, worried.

ANGELINA: (*Makes a sobbing sound.*)

GAIL: Right. So it really shows that she's scared. Well, she could have said, um,

ANGELINA (*speaking over Gail*): "She was scared."

GAIL: "Sundara was scared." Right. Would that have been interesting if she'd put it that way?

SYLVIA: No.

MARÍA (*speaking over Sylvia*): No.

ANGELINA: And I also liked the part where they say, "Oiee!"

GAIL: (*Chuckles.*) Right, right.

It was clear that the students understood the power of description as a means to captivate readers. As this excerpt also illustrates, Gail built upon the students' thoughts by offering another example to illustrate the point that they were making.

Time to Reflect

At the end of each LSC, the group debriefs. All participants, both students and the teacher, share their insights, commenting on what they learned from the discussion. This helps students move the discussion to a higher cognitive level, as it involves summarizing and synthesizing what they learned from the book and the discussion. Occasionally a student will say, "I didn't really learn anything," but this is very unusual. Often students will comment on what they learned from the content of the book—for example, from reading *Journey to Topaz* (Uchida), they may talk about how they learned about the internment of Japanese Americans during World War II, or from reading *Roll of Thunder, Hear My Cry* (M. Taylor), how they got to know more about racism and how it must have been to be African American in the 1930s. After discussing *The Gold Cadillac* (M. Taylor), Lance said, "Me, I learned that it's not always best to have a good kind of car. It's not always best to have something that is better than other people." Students will also comment on what they learned from each other; for example, in a discussion of *Stone Fox* (Gardiner), the group learned about customs and language surrounding death in the Tongan culture from Samesi, a peer who spoke about his mother's passing. Sometimes students will comment on what they learned about writing; on one occasion, Aromrack mentioned that she had learned how authors use words to paint pictures.

Because successful discussions require a lot of preparation and hard work on the part of all group members, it can be helpful to ask the question "What did you think about the discussion?" LSCs require strategies that students may not have much familiarity with (for example, directing questions at each other instead of to the teacher, really listening to what peers have to say, building on others' comments, feeling comfortable with having and expressing a different opinion from others, providing evidence to support a point of view, knowing when to listen and when to offer a comment, and knowing how to draw in less verbal members of the group). When students reflect on the success of the discussion, they often comment on their own and other students' participation during the discussion. In fact, Gail asks students to formally assess their preparation for and participation in LSCs by using a simple system of symbols: a plus sign means that the student shared an opinion and contributed to the overall discussion; a check mark means that the student only shared an opinion; a minus sign means he or she did not share. Students also comment on the degree to which the discussion was interesting. Gail also comments on what she noticed and appreciated. For example, at the end of a discussion about *The Gold Cadillac* Gail said, "I liked the way you asked for clarification. I really like your attitude when there's something that you don't understand and you come to the group and say, 'Can you help me? I don't understand this.'" After evaluating how well the discussion went, the participants may then suggest what they could do to improve the discussion the next time (for example, "Put notes in my book so I can find the pages," "Share my opinion even though it's the same as someone else's."). These debriefing sessions are very short, rarely lasting longer than two or three minutes.

The Teacher's Role

The teacher's role in LSCs is not what we may associate with literary discussions in high school or college. Instead of "teaching" a book, the teacher explores it with students. Throughout our own lives as students we usually sat passively while the teacher expounded on the meaning of the text. The teacher's role as the source of knowledge was sometimes disguised through a discourse style that seemed open-ended: the teacher would ask leading questions and students would then try to come up with the "correct" answer. The role of the teacher in a LSC is very different, and requires practice. We need to learn to share our own opinions, experiences and reactions to a book, but without dominating a discussion. We need to learn to follow the lead of students. Sometimes, this means that we have to put our own interests on hold. We need to learn to trust that students have thoughtful, intelligent, and interesting insights into books.

Sometimes we misread the intent of students' comments. For example, on one occasion a group of students and Gail were discussing *Children of the River*. The students were very animated when discussing the difficulties that Sundara, the main character, experienced as she moved between her home culture (Cambodian) and the school culture. Gail wondered if their animation was a reflection of their own cross-cultural experiences, as all the students in the group were children of immigrants. In fact, she was convinced that, while they were talking about Sundara, they were really talking about themselves. She therefore asked them to think about how the cross-cultural issue affected them. To Gail's surprise, the students indicated that they didn't feel that they had similar experiences:

ANGELINA: It only happened, it probably, it must happen so much, sometimes, but not often because Mexicans, they're almost like Americans—
SYLVIA (*interrupting*): Yeah. No, not really, not really.
GAIL: Can you think of any examples in your own cultures how you're sometimes caught between the Mexican culture and—
ANGELINA: Um, oh, yeah. In Mexico sometimes, in Mexico, they dress differently than here.
GAIL: But how about just now, even living here with your own family, how it's different than—
SYLVIA: Not really.
ANGELINA: The foods, the music. The music is really loud in Mexico. (*Other students agree with her.*)

Clearly this was not an issue the students were particularly interested in discussing. Angelina was very obliging, however, when Gail kept prodding ("But how about just now . . ."), by mentioning food and music. Angelina seemed to be searching for something to satisfy Gail. It was at this point that Gail realized that, although the issue was of great interest to her, it was of very little interest to the students, so she did not pursue it further.

While it is hard for teachers to assume a different role in discussions, it is also hard for students, particularly if they have been used to seeking out answers that the teacher is looking for. Also, even though we may tell students that we are equal participants, students may still give more weight to what we say. So, while we do share our opinions and reactions, we usually wait until all the students have shared so as not to influence their opinions. One of the first lessons we learned was to restrain ourselves from commenting on everything that students said.

At first, teachers may find it difficult not to constantly fire comprehension questions at students. When Gail first started LSCs, she felt compelled to ask such questions in order to assess whether or not the students really understood the book. This method of teaching was so ingrained in her that it wasn't easy for her to take on a more participatory role. In a letter to Katharine, Gail reflected on her development from inquisitor to facilitator:

> In the beginning, in spite of my training in LSCs, I found myself firing questions at the students. I sometimes thought that the students didn't understand the book, so by asking these questions, I thought I was helping them deepen their understanding of the book. There were times when the students needed something clarified, but other students were just as capable of providing insights into the book. What I realized was that this type of question/answer interrogation could not lead to a meaningful discussion, and perpetuated the idea that the teacher is the holder of all knowledge, that the teacher's opinion is the "right" opinion. This attitude really stifles discussion. Another difficulty for me was trying to overcome my uneasiness with silence. I found myself, the second no one was talking, wanting to fill the "void" with a question. Again, silence is an important part of having a dialogue. It provides think time and time for students to reflect on what their classmates have said. As teachers, we often do not give enough time to think.

As teachers learn to listen attentively and be coparticipants, they sometimes become completely silent, and never share their own insights or opinions. It is almost as if they are listening in on a discussion. There seem to be stages through which teachers go as they become increasingly familiar with LSCs. At first, they continue to dominate the discussion. Then they remain silent throughout the discussion, assuming that they shouldn't say anything. Finally, a more balanced stage evolves, where teachers listen and follow the discussion, but also offer their insights, reactions, and opinions.

During discussions the teacher should be alert to whether all students have had an opportunity to speak. The ones who have not spoken may be invited to share their opinions (for example, "Manual, was there anything you wanted to add?"). During the discussion students may be asked to elaborate on their comments in order to deepen understanding (for example, "Viliphone, what do you mean when you say that this book is better than *Iggie's House*?").

We are both still learning how to be more effective LSC co-participant-leaders, even though we are now comfortable with silence and with following and building on issues raised by the students. The type of LSC that we describe in this book involves a teacher who acts as co-participant, knowledgeable reader, and mentor. The teacher, while being a co-participant in the discussion, must at the same time be a guide or facilitator. Finding the balance between being a co-participant and being a facilitator takes practice, patience, a reflective stance, and a genuine interest in students' experiences, beliefs, and opinions.

Modifications for Inexperienced Readers

All children should have the opportunity to join an LSC, not just more fluent readers. If there's anything we've learned from the students' evaluations of LSCs, it is that they all prize these discussions. To deny a student access to these rich times of sharing because of a lack of fluency as a reader is counterproductive. Therefore, struggling readers should be given help.

Gregory was such a student. He avoided reading. He would focus on decoding, reading word for word. When Gail talked with him about what he had read, it was clear that he had not been reading to make meaning. He had been placed in remedial reading programs over the years, where the focus of instruction was on finding the subparts of language and reading decontextualized pieces of text. These classes seemed to underscore the notion that Gregory was incapable of being a reader. They certainly did not introduce him to the pleasures of books and reading, and, as a result, he frequently stated that he hated to read. Clearly, Gregory needed some positive experiences with books where he could see himself as an intelligent, successful student. Gail arranged for an adult volunteer to read the LSC books to Gregory so that he could join a group and be an active participant in discussions. Although he was not able to read the texts alone, he was able to discuss them articulately. As Gregory saw how books could lead to stimulating and enjoyable discussions, he seemed to relax and gain confidence in his ability as a reader, and he began to try to read the books on his own. Through the LSC discussions, Gregory was able to see that texts are to be understood and enjoyed, not simply decoded.

When upper grade teachers consider implementing LSCs, they often ask us what to do with students who have difficulty reading, like Gregory. We have found that the following strategies help.

Find a Buddy to Read With

One day Gail noticed that two friends, Roberto and George, were reading their LSC books together aloud. George was a very proficient reader, whereas Roberto struggled. They had chosen to read the same book and had come upon a very successful strategy that allowed Roberto to understand the book and later join in the discussion. Gail is not sure how this partnership developed and who initiated it, but it worked. She watched George read the pages aloud to Roberto and saw them discussing the book as they went along. She saw how excited Roberto was about the book. After reading three or four books with George, Roberto began reading books on his own. Later, he commented on his evolution as a reader over the year:

> I have changed because now I understand the book I read. For example at the biginning of the year I used to just read read but wouldn't understand the book so when they asked me questions

I wouldn't anwer because I wouldn't no the answer to the question. But now I read and follow along and I could understand
now so if they ask me a question I could answer it because I now
the answer.

Reading aloud with George offered the support Roberto needed in order
to become a more confident reader.

Lance was another inexperienced reader. He seemed overwhelmed by
the length of the books. He also found paired reading to be helpful. When
asked to reflect on how he had changed as a reader since the beginning
of the year, Lance wrote:

> I have really change. Now I could finish my book on time. I read
> every day. I started to change when I started to read with Dam-
> longsong. We would read 2 chapters in class and 2 chapters at
> home. We do that all the time. And I also improved in reading.
> I use to read slow but I read a little bit better now.

Lance and Damlongsong developed a system whereby they checked in
with each other on a daily basis. They also talked with each other before
selecting LSC books so that they would get the same book.

Roberto and Lance are two examples of students who solved their
problems independently. However, other students may need help from
the teacher. Sometimes paired reading involving peers does not work out.
For example, Antoine was having difficulty reading, so Gail asked Kadedra if she would be willing to read with him. Kadedra agreed to help, but
it was obvious that Antoine felt self-conscious. He would gaze around the
room, fidget, and talk with other students while Kadedra was reading to
him, which sometimes caused her to become impatient. We have learned
from situations such as these that it is important to ask the less fluent
readers if they would like peer support and, if so, with whom they would
like to read.

Read with an Adult

With some students, an adult partner works best. Gail enjoys having other
adults in the classroom, as this provides more individualized attention to

students. In any given week, student teachers, instructional assistants, or volunteers may be working with her students. One volunteer, Ginger, came to the class three days a week during the block of time devoted to language arts and read to a small group of three boys, all of whom were struggling readers. In advance of the whole class booktalk, Gail would let them know which books would be offered. The boys would then decide together on which LSC book they would read with Ginger. Ginger would make sure that she had finished reading the book to them by the deadline for the first LSC session. In this way, the three were able to participate in the discussion.

Offer Shorter and Less Complex Books

With less fluent readers who are reading on their own, the type of books that are offered for LSCs is particularly important. The selection needs to include shorter and less dense books that still appeal to older readers. Gail used to think that picture books would be inappropriate for her upper grade students as she felt they did not have much depth or complexity. However, since she has become more familiar with picture books, she realizes that this genre can provide all readers, especially the inexperienced reader, with a very successful experience with books. While it is true that many picture books, with their complex sentence structure and extensive vocabulary, may not be particularly easy to read, the illustrations and short texts make them more accessible to older readers who are struggling. Two books containing lots of pictures and a shorter text that have worked well for Gail's students are *JT* (Wagner) and *The Hundred Dresses* (Estes).

Have Books on Tape Available

Many novels are now available on tape, and we have found that some inexperienced readers become more engaged when they have the support of the tape while reading the book. This seems to be particularly helpful to students who are easily distracted, as the tape helps them focus their attention. Some students have enjoyed taking a tape recorder, tape, and book home; we have heard that other family members have enjoyed the stories, also. (The tape, however, should not be an excerpted or abridged version of the book.)

Modifications for Students Acquiring English as a Nonnative Language

The majority of students in Gail's class are nonnative speakers of English. Some of them are proficient in English and comfortable reading novels in English, whereas others are still acquiring English and are more comfortable using their primary language. We want all students to be active participants in discussions, so we welcome their comments in either English or their native language. In one discussion about *Children of the River,* Muang was whispering in Mien to Choulaphone. Gail asked Choulaphone to translate what Muang had said, and Choulaphone did: "She say if she were [Sundara] she would cry." Muang then began speaking loudly in Mien while looking at Choulaphone and the other students sitting beside her. During this discussion, Muang dissolved into tears from time to time. From Choulaphone's translations, it was clear that the book reminded Muang about her own experiences as a refugee fleeing a war-torn country. Despite her lack of fluency in English, she was an active participant in the conversation and was able to steer the discussion in directions that were important to her. At one point, Choulaphone told Muang in English that it was her turn. Muang said, "Wait" in Mien. It was apparent that Muang was pulling her thoughts together. When other students asked for a page number to correspond with her point, Muang responded in English, "Wait." Then she spoke in Mien, and Choulaphone translated for her:

CHOULAPHONE: She said that on page four and five. She say if she was Sundara she'd stay in Cambodia and let them kill her because she was [would be] so scared. She wants to stay in her country [She would want to stay in her country].

KADEDRA: She wanna stay with her family.

VILIPHONE: Why does she want them to kill her?

(*Muang speaks in Mien.*)

CHOULAPHONE: She say when she wait for her family to come [she wouldn't leave her country without her family].

VILIPHONE: But Sundara didn't know about the war yet, so how could she stay with her family?

(*Muang speaks in Mien.*)

CHOULAPHONE: If you love your family you don't go.

This excerpt from a discussion involving students who are new to English (Muang and Choulaphone), fluent nonnative speakers of English (Viliphone), and native English speakers (Kadedra), illustrates several points that we feel are important to consider:

1. The student's native language should be respected and students' contributions in the native language should be valued.
2. The degree to which a student is comfortable speaking English should be respected. In the case of Muang, she understood quite a bit more in English than her oral production would suggest; however, she was allowed to select the language in which to converse, thereby allowing her time to process and internalize English and build self-confidence.
3. Other students can act as translators, even when translation is difficult for them.

What was striking to us about this discussion was that, although *Children of the River* is a very long and complex book, Muang and Choulaphone had elected to read it, despite the fact that they were far from fluent in English. This book had been extremely popular in the class, and they knew that it was the only LSC book that addressed the experiences of Southeast Asian refugees. This seemed to be a major factor in their choosing the book. For example, Choulaphone translated for Muang, saying, "She didn't want to read this book because it's so long and hard." Gail asked her why she had picked such a long book, and Muang's response made it clear that the content influenced her choice. Choulaphone translated for her:

CHOULAPHONE: When her family was little and her mom tell her about what they did.
VILIPHONE: They should have a movie about this.
PHONESAVANH: She feels like she's there when her parents are telling her about Laos.

This conversation underscored for us how important content is. If we offer books that are meaningful and interesting to students, they are likely to read them in spite of any difficulties relating to fluency in a language.

Strategies that are effective with inexperienced readers also work well with children who are acquiring English as a nonnative language. We have learned to make sure that LSC selections include shorter books, books with lots of pictures, and books that address issues that students are familiar with. Some of the books that have worked particularly well with students acquiring English include *The Hundred-Penny Box* (Mathis), *Molly's Pilgrim* (Cohen), *The Hundred Dresses* (Estes), *JT* (Wagner), *Just My Luck* (Moore), *Fantastic Mr. Fox* (Dahl), and *Trouble with Magic* (Chew).

When there are several students who share a common language in which they are literate, books written in their native language may be offered. For example, one year Gail's class included several Spanish-dominant students. Gail located books in Spanish and gave students the option of reading books in English or Spanish. A Spanish-speaking instructional aide then led LSCs in Spanish.

Classroom Management

One of the most common questions that we hear from teachers who are interested in implementing LSCs is "What do the rest of the kids do while you are talking with one of the groups?" Students have several options during the reading period. They can read independently. They can read their LSC book. They can read picture books in preparation for buddy reading, a cross-age reading program (see Samway, Whang, and Pippitt 1995). They can write in their literature logs. They can complete the assignment for a second or subsequent LSC session. Although students have considerable leeway about how they use their time, they must use it productively, avoid disturbing others, and be ready for the LSC discussion deadlines.

Although a quiet environment is needed, total silence is not. It is important for readers to spontaneously share their reactions to a book with someone else. Basically, the environment should be quiet enough to foster thinking and reading. It is fine for students to talk about books with each other in a nondistracting way; but it is not fine if students are not using their time wisely and are distracting others. At the beginning of the year, Gail carefully monitors how students use the independent reading time. She pays attention to which students are engrossed in books and which are easily distracted. In the latter case, she notes what page the students are on to see if they are making progress. She talks with students, asking them how they are doing and if they are having any problems. Sometimes she sits down with students and helps them organize their time by breaking up the reading into reasonable segments so that they will be prepared for the discussion.

Right from the very first day, we make sure that students have a range of interesting and challenging learning events and activities so that they can work independently. We make it clear that we need to be able to concentrate on the discussion, which means that students cannot interrupt us and need to behave responsibly. When students are new to this type of freedom, we keep discussions short and move around the classroom, checking in with students. Although there are times when we wish we could simply focus on the discussion, we know that we have to be in touch with everything else that is going on in the classroom. A simple and unobtrusive way to do this is to sit at a table facing the rest of the class. In this way, eye contact and short verbal reminders can be used when students are not behaving appropriately.

Most students are not distracted by the discussion itself and are able to continue with their own work. Sometimes they listen in on another discussion (we do not discourage this, as it offers another literary experience). If students are distracted by the LSC discussion, they are encouraged to work in a separate, quieter area that is divided from the main part of the class by a partition. Usually, the children who cause disturbances are those who are the least experienced, struggling readers. They need appropriate and adequate support so that they can get into a book and be prepared for a discussion.

Some students finish reading their books quickly because they take them home and read at night, often into the early hours of the morning, if they are particularly engaged. It is therefore not uncommon for some students to finish a book in two days. It is best not to allow too much time to pass before meeting with a group. Students who finish reading their book several days before the meeting date and move on to other books should be encouraged to return to their literature logs to refresh their memory. In our experience, the students who are in this situation tend to be fluent readers who can read more than one book at a time. They are able to move back and forth between books reasonably well, as long as they have time to refresh their memories before a discussion.

Students quickly appreciate the opportunity to read and talk about books in class, and this has a positive effect on how readily they become absorbed in their books. The fact that students have to have finished a book in order to join the discussion motivates them to use their time wisely and appropriately. Once they have discovered the pleasure of having an intense, enjoyable discussion with their peers, they are much less likely to waste time or behave inappropriately. As in any classroom, successful LSC classroom management combines relevant and interesting curricula with reasonable and clear expectations for appropriate behavior (with consequences for inappropriate behavior). Sometimes, of course, there are problems. Depending on the child and the circumstances, the solution could be to separate students, to have them move to a quiet area, or to keep them in at recess, lunchtime, or after school so that they may complete their work. Students should be included in identifying and solving problems, and they should be consulted when evaluating classroom events. In such whole class meetings, students often raise issues that concern everyone in the class. These meetings also allow problems to be addressed collaboratively.

Gail had problems and questions when she first introduced her class to LSCs, but what sustained her was the students' excitement about reading and discussing books. One day, Marilyn proudly exclaimed, "This is the first chapter book I ever read." One morning, Vanessa, a student who was continually having problems in school and was often suspended, ran up to Gail in the hall and asked, "When are we going to meet and discuss our book?" These are not isolated comments; they are typical of students' reactions to LSCs.

In this chapter we have shared a variety of strategies that we have used in implementing literature study circles. With each group of students with whom we work, we make modifications, rethink our practices, and try to ensure that this experience with books is enjoyable, meaningful, and thought-provoking for the students—and for us. We have touched on the impact of LSCs on students' literacy development and understanding of other cultures. In the following chapters, we address these issues in greater detail.

 Chapter 3

"I Really Like Reading After All": The Influence of LSCs on Students

B OTH of us are readers, and over the years books have brought us great pleasure and introduced us to experiences and worlds that we might never have known otherwise. Our hope is that children will have similar enthusiasm for books.

Although some students begin the year as prolific readers, many more have had few successful experiences with books. This situation has been changing at Hawthorne School as teachers have moved toward literature-based reading programs in which students are given opportunities to enjoy books. The fear of books that we sometimes encounter among students has caused us to confer about what we can do as teachers to assist them in becoming more confident and successful readers. We know that it involves providing time in school for reading—lots of time, the kind of time that allows readers to become absorbed in a text. We know that it means giving students opportunities to talk about books with others in free-ranging conversations where different reactions to and interpretations of a text are welcomed. We know that it involves far more than completing worksheets and doing well on a norm-referenced "reading" test. We have always been concerned when students have said that they hate to read or consistently say they don't know what or how to read. Since working together in implementing an LSC program, however, we have seen how this single classroom activity has produced dramatic results.

In this chapter we demonstrate how LSCs have had an impact on students, in terms of both improving their literacy and understanding themselves more. We rely heavily on the students' own words in exploring these issues.

How Students View Themselves as Literate People

In many classrooms children spend hours each week "learning how to read." Often they focus on the subparts of language, completing work-sheet after worksheet designed to enhance comprehension, word defini-tions, literary terminology (for example, plot), and word attack skills (for example, root words, prefixes). In many cases, children may not read a book for more than five to fifteen minutes each day, if they are lucky. In the past, most of the students who came to Gail's class had these types of experiences. We still find that many students who come from other schools and districts have not had a pleasant prior experience with books. These students often discover for themselves what reading researchers have been saying: in order to be a fluent and successful reader, one has to read. Kadedra captured this insight in a written reflection: "When you read more you start to read better, and you want to read more, and you like to reading more, and [you] read faster." Monica also came to realize that the practice that is needed in order to become a reader involves read-ing a great deal. She wrote:

> At first I hated to read but the more I read the more I start to like it. So I guess it shows that if a certain person dislike to read, but they had to, and PRACTICE they would start to like it. You just have to have spirit. The more spirit you have the more you acom-plish things.

Katharine read Monica's reflection and asked her to explain a little more why she used to hate reading. Monica wrote back:

> See, I didn't like reading cause I never really paid much attention to it. It wasn't really my kind of thing. But then as I start to read more I start to get interested, so I liked it.

The kinds of experiences with books that Monica had had in the past removed the excitement and enjoyment that books can provide by reduc-ing the experience to a reading task rather than an engagement with text.

Being invited to read for the sake of reading, to read books that have been written to engage readers, and to have opportunities to talk about books with others can have a profound impact on students' reading habits and, consequently, on how they view themselves as literate people. Whereas they once hated to read and rarely read, they become enthusiastic and knowledgeable readers. Amphaivane was such a student. She used to read in school only, and even then she read reluctantly. At the end of sixth grade, reflecting on the impact LSCs had on her, she commented that she had begun to read at home and had read a large number of books, and that these accomplishments had altered her attitude toward reading and how she viewed herself as a reader. She wrote:

> The way I change about reading is that this year I read so many chapter books late [at night] and only reading chapter books has kind of change my life like on vacation I would stay up late and read a chapter book. I really like reading after all.

Travera, a fairly fluent but reluctant reader, commented on how LSCs had changed her reading behavior at home. She wrote:

> And sometimes when I'm at home I even want to read my book to my little sister if the book is real good and I feel proud of myself for doing that.

As this comment reveals, Travera's reading habits now include sharing "real good" books with family members, something she had rarely done in the past.

In trying to make sense of how students have changed as readers once they are introduced to LSCs, we have turned to their self-assessments. From them, we have learned that four features in particular have contributed to the children's growth:

1. Reading complete books.
2. Being exposed to books they may not otherwise have selected.
3. Reading a lot.
4. Being inspired to write.

Reading Complete Books

Over the years, we have noticed that many students in the upper grades never actually read a complete trade book or extended text. This is particularly true if reading instruction is grounded in textbooks, many of which, even those that are literature-based, rely heavily on abridged versions of, or excerpts from, trade books. In some cases, reading series rely on specially written stories that often lack the richness of trade books. This has helped us understand why so many students have told us that LSCs have led to their reading an entire book for the first time. We have been struck by the pride that students express when stating this accomplishment.

When students compare their former experiences reading textbooks with their more recent experiences with LSCs, they frequently comment on the limited nature of their textbook reading. Malcolm wrote, "Text books isn't really literature. Text books has bits of different books. The students want to read the whole book, not just one chapter." When Sean compared his former and current school reading experiences, he drew upon a metaphor in order to underscore the lack of satisfaction that he felt when reading the textbook stories. He wrote:

> When I would read Textbooks in grades 1–5 I would not like the storys. At best they were just the tip of the Iceburg and at worst they were boring and seemed like work for the sake of work. In Literature Studies Circles we got Intersting books with the whole story Included.

Later, when we talked with Sean, he expanded on his reactions to reading the literature-based textbook. He had enjoyed some of the stories and activities, he said, but was frustrated by the use of excerpts. In explaining his thinking, he drew upon another metaphor:

SEAN: Last year when I read *Festivals* [a reader in the Holt literature-based reading series], it was all right, in a way.

GAIL: How would you compare your last year, since you *did* read literature last year?

SEAN: Last year she read it to us, out loud, and that was a lot of fun, too. I liked doing the play. That was real interesting. And we talked a lot about it. I think it was almost, maybe just as good, but it was just different. And there were some parts, like the literature parts, that I think was just as good, but it was just different. And then the textbook, some of it I liked and some of it was . . . (*pause*). I can remember this story. I think it was called *And Now Miguel*, and I was reading that and it was neat, but then when it was over, it was over. It was an excerpt. And then a couple of [days] ago, maybe yesterday, I saw it.

GAIL: Did you read the book? So you read an excerpt from that book?

SEAN: Skeleton.

GAIL: A skeleton. Oh. And you didn't like it?

SEAN: I liked it, but it was—I liked parts of it, but parts of it was kind of missing.

GAIL: Did it motivate you to go and read the whole book? (*Sean shakes his head.*) Why not?

SEAN: Because all they've got is a skeleton. They don't have a heart and a brain or anything.

When students view reading as a chore, they often have difficulty engaging with books and do not become particularly independent or confident as readers. We have noticed how, in LSCs, students become more responsible and independent. This is most noticeable when they prepare for a discussion. They must take responsibility for finishing a book by the deadline. Even though the class discusses strategies for accomplishing that, students are ultimately responsible for their own preparation. The enticement of the discussion is usually enough to motivate them, and several students have commented on this change in their behavior as learners and readers. San Ching wrote the following in an end-of-year reflection:

How I change is I'm reading the whole book when the teacher want it to be done. In 5th grade I used to skip alot. But now I don't skip alot now I just try to finish. If I don't I will take it home and read it there.

If San Ching skipped a lot when reading in the past, he didn't actually read complete books, which he now does. Supra also commented on this phenomenon, while discussing how he now reads much more: "Before I was in the program, I couldn't even read one whole book to the end. The books that I picked were boring. But when I was in the program I got to read all types of books. . . . Now I'm reading more books than I ever did before." In explaining further how he changed as a reader, Supra wrote:

> I think I changed when our teacher started to do LSC. Before I'm used to reading short stories in a text book and not long books like Ms. Whang gives us. After I read two full books I started liking long books because I can imagine a more clearer picture then those text books.

As this reflection suggests, trade books can provide for an easier and more successful and satisfying reading experience because they are often more cohesive and better developed.

Several students have commented on how in the past they spent a great deal of time on just a few books. Kim Lon believed that reading the kinds of books that were available for LSCs and reading lots of books helped her as a reader. She wrote:

> It really improved my reading alot. And when I was at my old school I never read books like this. Of coures I check them out from the library, but not at school. We only read regular books, but if we read those books we've read only with the whole class and for last year we had finished only two books that why I liked this program.

Most of Kim Lon's exposure to books in school had been through textbooks and the occasional core reading book that was read by the entire class over many, many weeks. It is clear that she appreciated the opportunity to read lots of trade books and to read them relatively quickly and by herself, rather than as a whole class project. The fact that Kim Lon was a reader outside of school appeared to be unrelated to her former school experiences, something that Katharine could relate to, as she had been an avid out-of-school reader of books unrelated to her school reading, which, in junior and senior high school, was exam-driven and focused entirely on literary analysis. In fact, she remembers reading only one book for school that she enjoyed: William Golding's *Lord of the Flies*.

Being Exposed to Books That Students May Not Have Picked Up on Their Own

LSCs provide an effective way to extend students' reading repertoire by introducing them to books and authors that they may not read otherwise. In many cases, students commented to Gail on the length of books (for example, "This book was really long"), and then went on to tell how engaged they became. Linda Crew's *Children of the River* is a particularly good example of this phenomenon, as both its length and its small print initially deterred many students. In other cases, books that they may have put down quickly before, often because of a lack of action, dialogue, or mystery toward the beginning of the book, turned out to be favorites (for example, Natalie Babbitt's *Tuck Everlasting* and Mildred Taylor's *Roll of Thunder, Hear My Cry*). As students came to know authors and develop favorites, they would seek out other books by the same authors. When we noticed that students had particular interests or enjoyed a particular style, we would make recommendations.

Other students actively sought our recommendations. For example, Viliphone read *The Gift-Giver* (Hansen) and was enthralled with it. Even before the first LSC meeting, she approached Gail and said, "Ms. Whang, Ms. Whang, I love this book. Do you have any more by her?" Gail recommended that she read *Yellow Bird and Me* (Hansen), which Viliphone immediately began. In a similar way, Fahm began to seek out book suggestions from Katharine, with whom she corresponded in her literature log. One day she asked Katharine to share her own favorites: "Could you bring some book over that were written by your favorite author?" Katharine brought in *Julie of the Wolves* (George) and explained her selection in her letter to Fahm:

> Jean George has such an eye for detail. Her descriptions are so vivid that I feel like I am right there. I also like the strength of Julie's character—that's the kind of person I like. I wondered about how she would cope with being caught in two worlds— the world of Eskimos and the world of non-Eskimos.

Fahm immediately began to read the book, while also continuing to read other books, and referred to *Julie of the Wolves* in several letters to

Katharine. On one occasion, Fahm thanked Katharine for lending the book and told her how much she was enjoying it:

> I just wanted to say thanks for letting me borrow Julie of the Wolves. I started the book when you gave it to me. now I'm on page 46. I think by the time you get this letter I will be on page ninety eight. maybe it comes as a shock but I love to read. it gives me a chance to learn about diffrent things. Like Trouble with magic it gives me a chance to learn about magic.

Such opportunities to encounter previously unfamiliar authors and genres expand students' reading and experiential horizons. Because they are not required to read particular books, but can choose, they are more willing to read the books and are more enthusiastic in their responses. This is a reaction we can identify with. When friends lend us books or make recommendations based on their own enjoyment of a text, we are likely to read it, partly because we look forward to the shared experience that a good chat will provide.

Reading a Lot

When students compare their previous school reading experiences with LSCs, they frequently comment on how much they now read. Vanessa was not a reader when she entered Gail's class in sixth grade. However, she became an avid reader during her stay in the class. She attributed this dramatic change in her reading habits to the sheer act of reading lots of books. She wrote:

> When I first came to reading this year I hated it. Then in the middle of the year I started to like reading more and more because we used to have to read a [one] book after another. I started to like reading because when I [got] used to read[ing] I started to want to read more books like it.

Unlike many of the students who entered Gail's class, Travera was a competent reader. However, like many competent readers in our schools who do not have opportunities to read for authentic purposes, she rarely read. When reflecting on LSCs, she mentioned her pride in reading over one hundred books in the two years that she had been in Gail's class and commented on how this regular, independent engagement with books had enhanced her reading fluency:

> I think I can read real good and understand words in books. I think that sense [since] we read on our own I think I can read much faster than reading with other people. . . . What I think about the literature program is that it is good because you get a chance to read alot of books and I like doing that. I think it's better than reading the text books because you can read anytime you want and don't have to wait till the next day or till the teacher read the book again. I reaylled [really] enjoyed this program the two years I been in it because I've been able to read over 100 books and I feel proud of myself for reading that many books.

Most students' previous reading experiences have included many post-reading activities, which often take up more time than the reading itself. As students become more fluent and knowledgeable readers, they often remark unfavorably about these activities, particularly the endless questions and worksheets that are often assigned after reading. Monica's advice to teachers touched on the way in which reading can be either an enjoyable, involving, and revealing experience, or merely busywork ("just answering some questions"). She wrote:

> Teachers shouldn't use textbooks to much it's better to talk about it and learn than just answering some questions. Teachers shouldn't use textbooks because a chapter book seems more interesting and they have more methaphors. They also sometimes really get you in to the book. L.S.C. is getting into a circle . . . [to] talk about the book and share. Like the book *The Gift-Giver* it was about a boy and a girl being friends. It showed that a boy and a girl 'CAN" be just "FRIENDS". And that's it [It] doesn't go any further.

Monica realizes the importance of talking about books with others and, in the process, exploring human issues that are important to her—for example, that boys and girls do not always have to be romantically involved when they are friends.

Emery commented that LSCs had improved his reading "by reading more and reading faster also spending more times with books." This insight of his encompasses so much of what this section is about—that one needs to read, and read often, if one is to become a fluent reader, and that spending more time with books often leads to becoming a more engaged reader.

Being Inspired to Write

Sometimes students indicate that they want to embark on a project that is grounded in the book. We encourage them whenever this happens. For example, after reading *Children of the River*, a group of Mien and Laotian boys decided to write individual letters to Linda Crew. They wanted to know if she was planning a sequel, what other books she had written, and if *Children of the River* was a true story. They were thrilled when she wrote back to them (see Figure 9). She told them that she was not planning to write a sequel to this story (as many of them had hoped), and mentioned that she had been asked to write a short story about Asian characters. She invited the students to tell her about their lives, their problems, and stories about how they came to the United States.

After a long discussion, the boys decided to write their own stories. The letter exchange had generated in them an incredible energy, enthusiasm, and confidence that they could write their own stories, even though some of the boys were not fluent in English. The group discussed their experiences and options. Some, like Eata, wanted to write about their own and family members' experiences growing up in Laos. Eata brainstormed possible topics and embarked on a six-chapter book about Laotian customs, the first chapter of which he entitled "Ceremonies." In exploring wedding customs, he described the food that is brought to the wedding and how guests line up to be served:

> The other thing we do for the wedding is some people bring food for the wedding. They bring all kind of food. They make all kind of food. They even make fried pork skin. They have alot of fruit. They make fruit into beautiful decoration. My favorite decoration is the apple. They turn a regular apple into a swan. They also turn a watermelon into a basket with all kind of fruit inside it. . . . We only eat after the wedding. I don't really know why they do it, but it is a old costom. They get in a long line. The line was as long as three elephant. People keep coming for seconds and thirds

March 14, 1992

Dear Chansamone, Thanh, San Ching, Nopphavanh, Eata:

Thanks so much for writing to me. It was wonderful to get your letters and hear that you liked my book, CHILDREN OF THE RIVER. I got the idea for this book when a family of Cambodians came to work on our small farm here in Oregon. After we became friends with them, I realized they had many interesting stories to tell about their lives and how they had come to America. I realized that there weren't very many books about Southeast Asians, so I decided to try to write one.

 It wasn't easy for me to write this book because I'm not Asian and haven't actually lived through the experiences that you have. Before I even started to make up a fictional story, I studied for a whole year, reading everything I could find about Cambodia and interviewing different refugees. I wanted everything in my story to be absolutely authentic. Even though the characters in my novel and the things that happen to them are made up, everything is based on real situations. It was important to me that Asians would feel I was telling their story honestly. Because of this, there is nothing that makes me feel better than hearing from students such as yourselves who feel that the story "rings true"— (American expression!)

 At this point I am not planning a sequel about Sundara and Jonathan, but I have been asked to write a short story about Asian characters for a book to be used in schools. If any of you wanted to write and tell me about your lives and what's going on with you now, your problems, your story of how you came here, etc., I would love to hear from you. When I get letters such as the ones you already wrote, I always want to say, "Wait! What about *you?* What is *your* story?" I can't make any promises and of course I never put anyone in a book exactly as they are, but knowing what is going on with kids like you these days would help my next story be as authentic as possible.

 I'm glad you're all reading books. It's amazing how much you can learn about things just by reading good stories. Thanks again for writing to me. I appreciate it very much.

Sincerely,

Linda Crew

Figure 9 Linda Crew's letter

and they keep coming to get more. They have lots of Laos food at a wedding. It might be enough to stuff 1,000 people. I know because I've been to a laos wedding.

Other students were interested in retelling folktales from their native land. San Ching elected to do this and wrote several Mien tales. As we observed San Ching working on his stories over several weeks, we noticed that he was a more fluent writer of English than he was a speaker of English. He began a story about a turtle in the following way:

> Once upon a time there was a turtle and a women. One day the women was sleeping and she felt something on her. She woke up and saw the turtle on her. She didn't know, But the turtle mated with her. Soon she was pregnant and she got a baby turtle for a son. When the turtle grew up he saw the kings daughter and he wanted to marry her, but the king would not let him because he was a turtle.

In San Ching's story, the king gives the turtle a challenge he must meet in order to marry the princess (he is to find a two-week supply of food for the entire royal family). The turtle succeeds, marries the daughter, and lives happily ever after.

While these boys were writing and conferring, the rest of the class was fascinated by the evolving stories. It took the writers several weeks to complete their pieces; part of this time was spent gathering authentic details from family members. Up to this point, none of these students had shown much interest in writing. Linda Crew's response to their letters sparked a surge of interest in writing and exploring their own cultures. Her response had the effect of supporting and affirming their cultures, life experiences, and ability to write.

Greater Engagement with Books

We are impressed with the extent to which students who take part in LSCs become engaged by books, not wanting to stop reading, staying in at recess to read and talk about books, and reading until late at night at home. As they read, we hear them discussing what's happening in their books, or sharing their excitement with each other (for example, "Have you gotten to page 123 yet?" "Wait till you see what happens in the end!"). In addition, they begin to read more often at home, even though they have quite a lot of time in school to read. It is not uncommon to hear students comment on how they have sat in the bathroom at night reading so as not to disturb other family members with whom they share a bedroom. They also tell us how much they now enjoy reading during vacations and reading to younger family members. This kind of engagement with books is not often fostered by school-based reading activities, and we are delighted when it occurs. It reminds us of our own childhood experiences with books. For example, when Katharine was a child, she read under the bedclothes with the aid of a flashlight or crept into the bathroom late at night to finish a book that had engrossed her. As an adult Gail has often stayed up late to finish a book that has captivated her—and been exhausted the next day! Two factors seem to work together to facilitate this type of increased engagement on the part of the students: having choice over what they read, and having time to talk about books with others.

Choice

The impact of being able to choose what one will read appears in many of the students' comments when they assess their experiences with LSCs. Amphaivane talked about this in her written assessment:

> It's better then 1st–4th because now I get to choose my own books
> In 1st–4th I never had [the] chance to choose my own books, the teachers would shove a book in front of my face and [it] would be the book that they want me to read.

As Amphaivane so evocatively captures, there is a profound difference between being forced to read something and choosing what to read. Although the number of books available for each LSC selection is limited to four or five, thereby circumscribing the choices for students and the degree to which they are responsible for selecting books, there is sufficient choice for students to feel that they have some control. In contrast with school reading lists, which do not take into consideration students' interests and past reading experiences, LSC book choices reflect their interests and stretch them as readers.

Time to Talk About Books with Others

The impact of open-ended discussions that encourage students to express their opinions and reactions to a book, provide evidence to support their opinions, and ask questions of each other is dramatic—so dramatic that students frequently mention them, as Sylvia did when reflecting on how she had changed as a reader. She remarked on how the discussions influenced how she read books (she reads more carefully so as to be prepared for discussions) and how talking about books enhanced how she views herself as a reader (she is now much more confident):

> Well I have improved in my reading alot because I youse to never pay attention to the book all I did was read and read without knowing what the book was about. I have improved because now I talk alot in the conversation and I take alot of notes about the book alot of examples and I youse to never share. . . . I now believe in myself and I share as much as I want to. . . .

Even the most reticent students comment on how much they look forward to and appreciate the regular small group discussions that are at the core of LSCs. Rhodora compared these discussions with the kind of talk one has with friends after watching a movie. She wrote:

> I like [LSCs] because we get to express how we feel about the book. It's like watching a movie with all your friends. And after the movie everybody starts talking about it. Everybody tells how they feel about the movie, which part they didn't like, and what the producer should've done to make it intresting.

The type of excitement that Rhodora expresses we have observed over and over again in LSC classrooms. We hope that all young readers may have opportunities to experience the excitement that Rhodora has in reading.

Development of Reading Preferences

Even when students enter Gail's class as readers, they generally have a limited repertoire of genres and authors. In some cases, students are knowledgeable about a book series such as The Babysitters Club or Sweet Valley High series. At the beginning of the year, they often judge a book by its length, the number of pictures, and the amount of action in the plot. After being introduced to a wider selection of books through LSCs, many of which contain richly developed characters, themes, and plots, students' reading preferences are expanded. While they continue to read their old favorites, they also read more extensively and with a more critical eye. For example, when Quoc began the school year he judged the "goodness" of books by how much action was present. By the end of the year, however, he remarked how he had changed in his judgement of books and how this change had been influenced by the reading he did during the year:

> My Attitude changed when we started reading. It was boring because it had no exciting parts in the books Ms. Whang pick out. Now I like books better not for the excitment, but for how the Author descibes the setting.

He acknowledges that, at first, this was a hard transition to make, but once he got into the different kinds of books, he learned to appreciate more than action.

We regularly ask students to assess their classroom experiences. This allows us to gain insight into what is working or not working and why. Also, students are offered an opportunity to make book recommendations, which enhances their confidence and helps them articulate their reading preferences. Miguel had mixed feelings about the books that were available for LSCs. On the one hand, he liked LSCs "becaus there where soem of my faivrot athores." On the other hand, the selection had not been as satisfying "because no action books." He had particularly enjoyed *Maniac Magee* (Spinelli). Emery commented that he would have liked more "exiting thrilling books." Amphaivane apparently thought that Gail wasn't paying enough attention to student preferences, as she suggested that Gail ask for more recommendations from students. She wrote:

> What could be improve is to ask the students what type of book they could get into so that they would talk lots and lots more about it.

In other cases, students took the initiative and made recommendations to us. As mentioned earlier, Fahm had been corresponding about books with Katharine, and would often suggest that she read certain books: "Have you ever read trouble with magic because it's really exciting and I really loved the book." Fahm would borrow books from her classroom library to lend to Katharine, and Katharine would bring in books from her own collection for Fahm to read. At one point, she asked Katharine to tell her about her favorite authors. Fahm then took the initiative and shared her own favorites, telling why these were her favorite authors:

> Since you told me alot of you're favorite authors I'll tell you mines and why I like them. Ruth Chew, the reason I like Chew is because she writes about magic . . . Milderd D. Taylor and the reason I like Milderd D Taylor is because she writes about true story.

Later in the semester, Fahm came back to comment on a book that Katharine had lent her, *Julie of the Wolves*, and asked for more recommendations:

> By the way the book you let me borrow was really good. Do you have any another books you can lend me. I really like the book you lend me first well I hope you could?

This written conversation continued and, after Katharine had written about one of her favorite books, *The Eyes of the Amaryllis* (Babbitt), Fahm asked to borrow it:

> Did you finish The Eyes of the Amaryllis? if you did could I read it. it sounds rather exciting I espially love books with spooky places in it.

As students read a range of complete books for LSCs and discuss them with their peers and the teacher, their knowledge of books expand, they become increasingly more aware of their own likes and dislikes, and they become more resourceful during independent reading time.

Multiple Opportunities to Think Critically

In LSCs critical thinking is fostered in both open-ended discussions and in preparing for the discussions.

Open-ended Discussions

One of the most important elements in LSCs is the open-ended discussions. They offer students opportunities to explore books in ways that draw on their intellect and experience, unlike the skills sheets that often accompany reading sessions. Some of the students in Gail's class have had the life experiences of much older children, and this gives them a maturity that other children may not possess. LSCs allow them to integrate their life knowledge and school learning. For example, after one group of students had read *Scorpions* (Myers), which is set in an inner-city neighborhood and is about the pressure placed on a young boy to join a gang, they drew on their own knowledge of gang life and explored why young people join gangs and whether they have other choices available to them. They did not agree about what happens when a person wants to leave a gang, and this led to a long discussion about dealing with peer pressure and the sociopolitical origins of gangs.

The discussion around *Scorpions* was typical of many LSC discussions in that students had opportunities to express a point of view and disagree with each other. Sounthavy wrote, "Somthing I've learned form this program is that other kids may see things diffrent then me." That is, having time to talk about books can lead to enhanced understanding. Roberto wrote:

I have changed because now I understand the book I read. For example at the bigining of the year I used to just read read but wouldn't understand the books so when they asked me questions I wouldn't answer because I wouldn't no the answer to the question. But now I read and follow along and I could understand now so if they ask me a question I could answer it because now I now the Answer.

In addition to the open-ended discussions, which foster critical thinking, we also ask students to reflect on classroom events and practices, as we value their advice. Much of what we do as teachers is shaped by students' input. On occasion, students' comments indicate the degree to which LSCs provide for intellectual development. For example, when Somphone responded to our query as to what advice students would give to teachers who are new to LSCs, he commented on how LSCs allow for intellectual growth, what he referred to as "help their minds" and "become scholorship person":

> My advice for teacher's is that they should incourage their student into reading more paperback book that will help their mind's to read and learn. Such as learning metaphor's or learning dialoge and dialect. How they could become a scholorship person is by reading plenty of paperbacks. And another way to be a scholorship's is by cooperate in the Literature study circle by expressing their feeling's about the book and why they liked it and what so good about it.

Amphaivane also commented on how reading, talking, and intellectual development are intertwined. She wrote, "I learned that reading and sharing helps the mind improve."

The open-ended discussions allow for clarification and elaboration, both of which extend understanding. In the process of talking about a book, students often clarify meaning for each other. For example, at one point when a group of students was talking about *Children of the River*, the discussion focused on the way the author, Linda Crew, rendered the English dialogue of the Cambodian characters. Sylvia pointed out that one sentence in particular didn't make sense to her, referring to it as "spelling":

SYLVIA: I wonder why they have the spelling like that. They don't really pronounce. They go (*reading from the book*), "Maybe you could do again."

ANGELINA: Maybe you could do it. Do. (*Reads from the book.*) Oh, yeah, "You could do again."

SYLVIA (*reading from the book*): "You could do again."

ANGELINA: No, it's 'cause that's how Chinese talk, that's how many. That's how a couple of Cambodians talk when they get here. They're, they forget some words, or like stuff like that.

Clearly, Sylvia and Angelina were trying to figure out what was going on, and eventually Angelina concluded that the speech pattern was typical of the language of a recent, nonnative English-speaking immigrant to the United States.

Preparation for LSC Discussions

Preparation for the LSC discussions also offer students occasions to think critically. They use idea bookmarks and their literature logs to reflect in writing, both before the first discussion and when preparing for follow-up meetings.

For example, Angelina found the written reflection that students were asked to engage in very fruitful. She spent a lot of time writing in her log and on idea bookmarks. She was an active reader and discussion member. Interestingly, though, once she came to discussions, she rarely referred to her log or bookmarks. It was as if the written notes prepared her, but she was able to sustain her role in conversations without written support.

By the end of the year, the log was bursting with pages and it looked messy, though the colors on the front cover were still brilliant. It was the messiness that accompanies constant use. Corners of pages were dog-eared. Idea bookmarks were stapled throughout. Yellow post-its were piled one on top of the other on some pages. A quick glance in her log tells quite a bit about Angelina as a reader, writer, and thinker. It also reveals the range of literate activities that she was exposed to through LSCs. On the cover page, Angelina wrote "ANGELINA'S" in carefully formed shadow letters, purple highlighted in green. On the back cover she wrote across the bottom of the cover in green pen, "You need the brains to read a book and to actually understand what they are saying or what the subject is about so go out and buy a big brain tha[t] works." In red pen is the comment, "Book are Good & Bad" (see Figure 10).

In the back of the log is a list of books that Angelina read in one year, both for independent reading and for LSCs (see Figure 11). Although this list totaled fifty-two titles, she actually read more, as she wrote comments on books that she didn't list in the back of her log (for example, *Otherwise Known as Sheila the Great* by Judy Blume, *Roll of Thunder, Hear My Cry* by Mildred Taylor, *Lupita Mañana* by Patricia Beatty, *Child of the Owl* by Laurence Yep, and *Welcome Home, Jellybean* by Marlene Fanta Shyer). In addition to the title and author, Angelina's log rates each book: a minus sign for "bad"; a check mark for "OK"; a plus sign for "great";

Figure 10 The back cover of Angelina's log

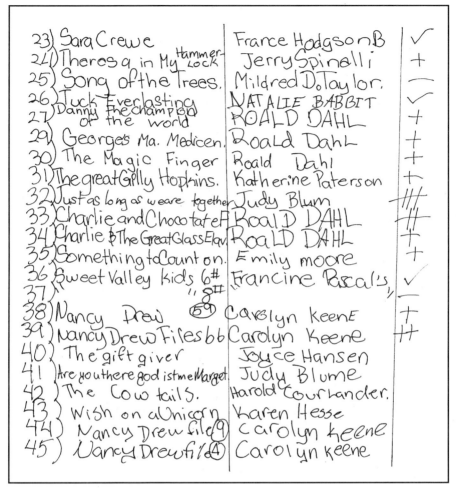

Figure 11 One page from Angelina's list of books

and two plus signs for "double great." She began the year reading several Judy Blume books, all of which she rated as "great." One of these, *Iggie's House,* she read for LSCs. She then read eighteen books in the Babysitters Club series, five of which she rated "great," four "bad," and nine "OK." None of these books were LSC choices, but the fact that she read so many indicates the degree to which she was hooked on the series and was a prolific reader.

Angelina frequently made predictions as she was reading a book. For example, while reading *Sara Crewe* (Burnett), she wrote:

pg. 69 I thought that Miss. Minch was going to get so greddy and mean with Sara that she was going to throught away her new clothes and stuff she was getting.

When reading *Tuck Everlasting* (Babbitt), she predicted what would happen to the mother if the Man in the Yellow Suit were to die; in the process of making this prediction, she seemed to be arguing with herself, forcing herself to think through her argument more fully:

Pg. 64 I think that they are goign to hang Mea if [double underlined] the guy in the yellow suit dies from when Mea shoot at him, but she can't die then that would show that she knows were the spring is and they maite offer money to tell them were the spring is they mate torcher her and they will proabably torcher her so bad that that maite make her self die.

What is particularly striking about Angelina's written comments is the way that they appear to help her sort out her thinking. She thinks while she reads. She asks questions and answers them for herself, thereby gaining clarity. She raises issues that confuse her (for example, "Pg. 64 This part really confused me because they were talking about the wheel and then they started to talk that they stole there horse").

Angelina also commented on authors' literary styles. She liked to get into the meat of a book quickly and wasn't very tolerant of authors who set up the story through a lot of description (for example, "Pg. 62 Too much description that it makes it boring"). She read the Nancy Drew series, which she really enjoyed, and after reading *Secret in the Old Lace* (Keene), she wrote:

I love this book becaus it is soooo Mysteryes and many books don't start with the mystery until almost the middle, and it makes you not want to read any more.

After Gail introduced students to idea bookmarks as an alternative to writing in the logs while reading the book, Angelina used them regularly, often writing multiple thoughts on a particular book. For example,

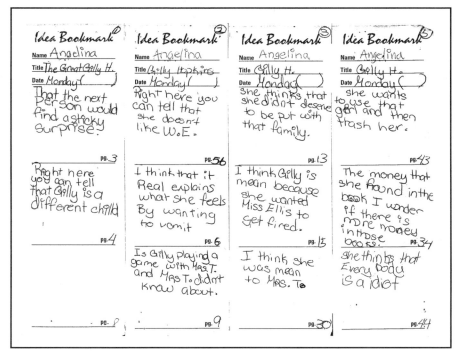

Idea Bookmark ①
Name Angelina
Title The Great Gilly H.
Date Monday ( )
That the next
person would
find a sticky
surprise.
                    pg. 3

Right here
you can tell
that Gilly is a
different child

                    pg. 4

Idea Bookmark ②
Name Angelina
Title Gilly Hopkins
Date Monday ( )
Right here you
can tell that
she doesn't
like W.E.
                    pg. 56

I think that it
Real explains
what she feels
By wanting
to vomit
                    pg. 6

Is Gilly playing a
game with Mrs. T.
and Mrs. T. didn't
know about.
                    pg. P

Idea Bookmark ③
Name Angelina
Title Gilly H.
Date Monday ( )
She thinks that
she didn't deserve
to be put with
that family.
                    pg. 13

I think Gilly is
mean because
she wanted
Miss Ellis to
get fired.
                    pg. 15

I think she
was mean
to Mrs. T.
                    pg. 30

Idea Bookmark ④
Name Angelina
Title Gilly H.
Date Monday ( )
She wants
to use that
girl and then
trash her.
                    pg. 43

The money that
she found in the
book I wonder
if there is
more money
in those
books.
                    pg. 34

She thinks that
Every Body
is a idiot
                    pg. 44

Figure 12 Four of Angelina's nine bookmarks about **The Great Gilly Hopkins**

when reading *The Great Gilly Hopkins* by Katherine Paterson, Angelina
used nine idea bookmarks (see Figure 12). The entries show her thinking
while reading the book. She used her log to offer advice to the teacher
and her fellow students:

> I think that this book was really good, but I think that if the
> teacher would have given us a litte more time it would have been
> better so next time that the teacher puts a book to read finish
> before it is due.

This comment suggests that Angelina regarded the log entries as an opportunity to inform her teacher about a problem and suggest a possible
solution.

Lupita Mañana (Beatty) was one of the few books that Angelina read
that was grounded in her own family's culture. It is about a sister and

brother who come to the United States without documentation in order to find their supposedly rich aunt. She loved this book, was completely engaged, and wrote twenty-four separate comments about the book on idea bookmarks as she read it, more than she did for any other book (Figure 5 on Page 43 gives a sampling of her comments). On some of the bookmarks she asked questions:

> Leaving the children, Lupita came back to the door, which she had left "ajar." What does "Ajar" mean. Pg 21
>
> She was covered with gooseflesh. What is gooese flesh? Pg 177
>
> What is that game "jaialai." I have never heard of it. Pg 52
>
> Does Pocho mean born in the U.S.A. and your parents were born in Mexico. Were did that word come from? Pg 25

A lively discussion had centered on the meaning of *pocho* during the LSC, but the group could not agree on its meaning.

Angelina also made inferences, as when she wrote, "They wanted to dress Lupita as a boy so that well I think she wouldn't get Raped." And she related the story to her own roots in Mexico: "On the hill side of my town in Mexico poor people some times they are so many that the town gets bigger every year! Pg 18." She stated her opinion, as when she wrote the following comments:

> They called Mexicans with out papers "Aliens" How rude
>
> I hate Salvador he is such a jerk he doesn't care for her no more
>
> I think that she should learn inglish and she will never get caught. They don't look at your papers

The degree of affective and literary engagement that Angelina demonstrated with regard to *Lupita Mañana* (Beatty) carried over to many other books—for example, *The Star Fisher* (Yep), which she read after *Lupita Mañana*. Her entries for *The Star Fisher* reveal a similar range of responses. For example, she continued to ask questions ("What does bosom mean it doesn't sound like a fimiliar word"). She also indicated that she was unsure of the book's purpose: "I didn't really under stand the story I didn't get the plot of the story."

The degree to which Angelina regarded reading as a thinking process is reflected in the examples that we have shared from her log and idea bookmarks. The open-ended nature of the writing gave her opportunities to explore issues that intrigued, puzzled, and concerned her. This type of critical thinking is something that is fostered in many students as they engage with books in LSCs. This is the kind of reading experience that we hope all young readers have.

Frequent Opportunities for Students to Define Themselves

Books can have a profound impact on how we view the world, how we interact with others, and how we feel about ourselves. That is, books can help us define who we are. On occasion, students have remarked that they have been changed in profound ways by a book (and also by the discussions that accompanied its reading). For example, Fahm was a painfully shy girl who rarely spoke up, even in small group discussions. One day, she revealed in her journal how reading *The Shimmershine Queens* (Yarbrough) had led to her being more willing to speak up for herself:

SPEAKING UP
The book that help me the most was Shimmer Shine Queens because it talks about a girl standing up for herself and saying what she thinks and the way she help me was that she stuck up for herself she spoke alot and after I read this book I learn how to speak up more and I learn how to say what I think a little more. . . . So this book really help me alot because after I read this book I spoke up a little more, and I stood up for myself. And even when I'm out side I still stand up for myself because if you don't then the people that says things to you that hurt your feelings then there going to keep doing it because their going to think that you can't do anything about it. . . . I think that the girl in Shimmer Shine Queen really help me change alot because even though I don't speak alot inside the classroom I still speak and it's better than just sitting and not doing anything.

Dien, another reserved student, also commented on how the same book gave her (and other students) the courage to speak up:

> I liked . . . Shimmer Shines Queen because it was the book that gave me courage to speak up in the discussions because this girl in the book was scared of another girl but finally at the ending she stood up for herself. And that was the first discussion that we wer'nt scared to speak up and while we were reading, it all gave us a feeling to speak up.

This greater sense of self-confidence continued throughout the year for Fahm and Dien, two girls who had great difficulty asserting themselves. In order to support them, Gail would sometimes remind them not to forget the "shimmershine feeling." It was a special code they used with each other throughout the year. Sometimes, one or both girls would run up to Gail on the playground or in the classroom and proudly announce that they were practicing the "shimmershine feeling."

In other cases, books helped students deal with their everyday lives. For example, Travera found books helpful when confronted by problems at home, as they often offered her potential solutions and different perspectives from those she had previously considered. She remarked in her journal how this knowledge allowed her to support family members who may not have thought through a situation as well as she would have liked:

> How the books and reading discussions has helped me with problems is that when I go home and hear problems that I read in books is that I tell my family I think I know a way to solve the problem. I also tell my cousins that when you get asked to be in a gang think about it and think about all the things that happen when your in a gang because theres alot of risks to take when your in a gang. Thats what I learned from books in the reading program.

As even a small school can seem overwhelming to a newcomer, it is not hard to imagine how overwhelming it must be to enroll midyear in a huge school like Hawthorne. Choulaphone read *The Kid in the Red Jacket* (Park), and it reminded her of when she first came to Hawthorne.

She commented on how reading this book had helped her overcome her shyness:

> The book that help me alot is when I was reading the Kid in the Red Jacket. This book reminded me when I first move to Hawthorn. This book is about a kid who just move to a new school and had no friends. And this book help me talk to other people when they talk to me. . . . I was really shy and scared when I first came to this school. I didn't know who to talk to. And after I finish the book I talk more, and this book helps me alot.

Darron may have been one of the students who made Choulaphone's transition to Hawthorne more difficult than it need have been. He has a strong sense of humor and tends to joke around and tease other students. In the course of the two years that he was in Gail's class, he read several books that touched on the negative aspects of teasing. At the end of his final year in the school, Darron commented on how reading certain books, such as Judy Blume's *Blubber*, had changed how he interacted with his peers. He wrote:

> When I was in the forth grade I used to teas about people alot but now that I have read some books that has teasing in them. I now know that teasing is a bad habit because you can hurt alot of peoples feelings.
>
> One of the books I read that has teasing was called Blubber. It tells how a girl got teased about her weight, her fatness, and how ugley she was. But then at the end those girls who teased her fanilly found out that how a person would feel if they got teased and they fanilly stop teasing her.
>
> So that why one of the main reasons a person should'nt teas is because if you teas and one day some thing that pops up on your face or some thing else happens you would'nt want other people to teas you. So that why now I don't teas so much.

Books and discussions enabled Darron to see that his actions and words could have a harmful impact on others, and he decided to monitor and change his style of interaction.

When we consider how books have moved us and altered our own views of the world, we should not be surprised to discover that the same is true for younger readers. Unfortunately, in too many classrooms this type of engagement with books is rare. With the move toward more literature-based reading instruction, children are more likely than in the past to read complete books. But this type of instruction provides no guarantee that students will engage in open-ended discussions that allow them to explore and develop their thinking. These discussions enhance the reading experience and increase the likelihood that books will have a profound impact on students. This is one of the most satisfying aspects of LSCs.

Chapter 4

"I Think I Might Have Been a Little Bit Racist Before Coming to Hawthorne": The Influence of LSCs on Cross-Cultural Understanding

Like other educators around the country, we are constantly exploring ways to incorporate students' backgrounds and cultures in order to build supportive and challenging learning environments. We have seen our fair share of conflicts that have arisen as a consequence of misunderstanding and prejudice. We have heard the racial slurs and name-calling that often punctuate playgrounds and classrooms. We have seen how linguistic differences can lead to misunderstanding. We have heard students chastising their nonnative English-speaking peers by saying, "Speak English, I can't understand you." We have heard students making fun of the pronunciation of emerging English speakers. We have also witnessed misunderstandings that are grounded in different styles of communication.

One day, Gail was talking with May Phou, a Mien student who had a problem with a boy who was spreading rumors about her. Throughout their discussion, May Phou never once looked directly at Gail. Instead, she looked to Gail's side, whether she was listening or talking. Gail listened to May Phou, but found herself getting agitated because May Phou was not making eye contact, a signal for Gail that one is listening. It occurred to Gail that perhaps the two of them had different approaches to speaking and listening. Later in the day, during a community circle discussion with the class, Gail mentioned her confusion over May Phou's lack of eye contact. Many of the Laotian and Mien students then explained how, in their cultures, it is considered rude to look adults in the eye when speaking to them, that looking down is a sign of respect. Thanh, a Laotian student, commented, "If I look at my parent eye, I will get in trouble." May Phou added, "We have to look down when we talk to our parent." During the discussion, Muang, another Mien student, commented that in the previous year a teacher had raised his voice at her and said, "Look me in the eye when I'm talking to you!" and that this had made her feel very uncomfortable. Tamara, an African American student, commented that in her house, it was different. She said, "My mother told me that I have to look at her when I'm talking to her." Through this discussion, the students learned that respect and listening are expressed differently from culture to culture. May Phou and Fahm learned that in some cultures eye contact shows respect and indicates that you are listening. Other students learned that if a Laotian or Mien student isn't looking directly at them, it does not necessarily mean that they are not listening.

Conflicts among students mirror those of the larger society. It is not easy to counter the prevailing mood in the nation, one of hostility toward others who do not share one's race, language, culture, or social standing. While the experiences we describe in this book are grounded in a particular community, the Fruitvale District of Oakland, California, conversations we have had with other educators in quite different communities tell us that similar cross-cultural difficulties exist throughout the country. The ethnic and linguistic makeup of classrooms may be different, but the underlying issue seems to be the same: ignorance often leads to prejudice.

We have both lived and worked in very different cultures from those in which we grew up. We have also experienced prejudice firsthand. Gail grew up in San Francisco in the 1950s. As a Korean American, she was one of just a few Asian Americans in her elementary and junior high schools. She was teased for looking different and was often called "Chinaman." She remembers her brother being punched when the Korean War broke out. Growing up in such a hostile environment, Gail felt ashamed of being Korean and was embarrassed by her grandfather and grandmother because they didn't speak English. In school, she never read books that portrayed people who looked like her. In addition, she never learned anything about the contributions of Asian Americans to the development and history of the United States. In fact, the contributions of Korean Americans hadn't been documented. As Gail and her Korean American contemporaries grew up, they started to ask questions, such as: Why is it that the only mention of Koreans in history texts is in reference to the Korean War? Why wasn't the history of the early pioneers documented? As an adult, Gail and her cousin, Brenda Paik Sunoo, became involved in an oral history project that helped piece together the missing history of Koreans in the United States. Through interviewing first generation Korean Americans and making slides of old photographs from the picture albums of the early pioneers, these third generation Korean Americans were able to reconstruct the lives and contributions of their Korean ancestors. Once self-conscious about her Korean heritage, Gail is now knowledgeable about and proud of it.

Katharine grew up in the 1950s and 1960s in the northwest of England. The prejudice she encountered was grounded in social class and the way she spoke. In England there are marked differences in how Northerners (or at least those who haven't taken elocution lessons or grown up in upper class homes) and Southerners pronounce words, and she speaks with a Northern accent. Until relatively recently, the way one spoke in England reflected one's social class, and social class generates its own brand of prejudice. She grew up being surrounded by reminders that those who spoke like Northerners were somehow inferior. Nobody in power spoke like her—not teachers; not radio announcers, not even those in regional radio; not professional people such as doctors or ministers. Public references to "correct" or "good" English underscored the notion that some people, usually from more humble homes, were inferior. The books Katharine devoured as a youngster, grounded as they often were in boarding school life and country mansions, rarely, if ever, reflected the realities that she encountered. When she was about thirteen, she decided to talk "posh" in school. This lasted only a few weeks, but it reflected Katharine's problem with self-image at that time. Even today, when she watches BBC shows on PBS, she notices that stupid, bumbling, or criminal people are often portrayed as Northerners, and she is reminded of how insidious prejudice is.

We have shared these personal anecdotes in order to explain, in part, why we both feel so strongly about the importance of creating inclusive classroom environments where differences are respected and celebrated. With an increasingly diverse student body, it is incumbent on all educators to design curricula and learning experiences that are relevant for all students, while also promoting understanding among people from different backgrounds. As Gail reflects on her own childhood experiences, she feels that the fact that she rarely saw positive images of Asian Americans in the media, in textbooks, and in literature affected her self-esteem and contributed to inferior feelings she had about herself. This experience is true of many ethnic groups who, in school, are assigned books mainly about Caucasian protagonists growing up in middle class neighborhoods. In order to make education relevant and meaningful to children today, literature that reflects the people and multiple perspectives present in the increasingly diverse, multicultural population of the United States must be included.

As our cities and schools become more and more culturally and linguistically diverse, classrooms begin to look like mini–United Nations. It is not unusual today to teach in a school where more than twenty languages are spoken. In one school in San Francisco, forty languages are spoken. The fifth and sixth grade students in Gail's classroom are members of many distinct cultural and ethnic groups. Some educators regard such diversity with trepidation, but we view it as a tremendous opportunity to learn about and appreciate differences. We believe that ethnic, cultural, and linguistic variation need not be the source of strife, as it so often is.

Most of the students presented in this book speak a language other than English. Very few of them, however, have had opportunities in school to maintain their home language while also learning English. They often feel torn between the demands of the dominant culture and those of their home culture. As educators, we feel that this is unacceptable. Being a member of more than one linguistic and cultural group should be viewed as an asset.

In LSC discussions, students have commented on the conflict that these unnecessarily divisive demands place on students. For example, during a discussion of *Children of the River* (Crew), the group was exploring ways in which Sundara was torn between her native Cambodian culture and her adopted American culture. The students began to talk about their own bilingualism:

MARÍA: When I'm here, I talk English and then when I get home, I want to talk English, too, and then my mom's like, "No, you're (*inaudible*)

SYLVIA (*finishing María's thought*): Eres Mexicana (You're Mexican).

MARÍA: And she's like, "You're Mexican, you know?" and I'm like, "So?" and I'm like (*chuckles*). She's all like, "Well, you have to talk Spanish 'cause—

ANGELINA (*interrupting*): You'll forget it.

MARÍA: I'm all, "Uh-huh, yeah, sure."

(*Several students are speaking at the same time.*)

MARÍA: In Mexico, I have a problem with my dad because he knows English. I'll talk to him in English, and my mom's like, "There's Mexicans here."

ANGELINA: Yeah. That's how my dad is. My dad won't let me talk English at my house. He says, "You'll forget! You'll forget how to speak Mexican." I'm like, "Oh, OK."

GAIL: He wants you to be bilingual.

ANGELINA: And then we go to Mexico and I'm forgetting English because I'm talking Spanish all the time.

As this excerpt shows, parents do not want their children to lose their native language. They want their children to be bilingual so that they may succeed in an English-dominant society while also being able to appreciate their cultural heritage and interact with family members and friends who are not fluent in English. The United States, unlike many other countries, has failed to take advantage of the huge multilingual capacity of its people. When multilingualism is not respected and sought after, children are caught in the kinds of dilemmas illustrated in the conversation above.

In many schools, multiculturalism and diversity are addressed only at specific times of the year (for example, Black History Month, Hanukkah) and/or only through a song or food (for example, singing songs in Spanish or preparing tacos on Cinco de Mayo). This short-term, activity-based approach to multicultural education is sometimes referred to as a tourist curriculum. While we believe that it is important to recognize and celebrate days and events that are special for different people, we also believe that multiculturalism should be infused in the curriculum throughout the year, not just on special days. We have found that exploring books with children in LSCs is one way to do this.

Although we do not limit the LSC selections to books that are obviously multicultural—such as Laurence Yep's *Dragonwings* (about Chinese Americans), Yoshiko Uchida's *Jar of Dreams* (about a Japanese American girl), or Candy Dawson Boyd's *Circle of Gold* (about an African American family), we have found that the open-ended LSC discussions often explore cross-cultural issues simply because of the diverse backgrounds of group members. Although the students share many experiences because they live in the same neighborhood, they also have different experiences, memories, and oral histories that they draw on in the discussions, including those grounded in culture, race, age, gender, social class, and geographical location. This means that we are likely to talk about issues that trouble and interest the students throughout the year, not just at Thanksgiving, during Black History Month, or on International Woman's Day.

Generally, during the first LSC discussion, students share their own affective responses to the book, what Rosenblatt (1978) refers to as an aesthetic response to literature. We often hear different interpretations of and perspectives on a single event in a story (for example, in Babbitt's *Tuck Everlasting,* whether Winnie made the right decision not to drink the magic water). We also hear students deriding customs that are outside their realms of experience (for example, the scene in *Children of the River* that describes a Cambodian girl showering in a school locker room with a towel wrapped around her). We hear students challenging an author's portrayal of characters (for example, the perceived racist portrayal of the elderly man in Theodore Taylor's *The Cay*). We see students trying to make sense of something that they consider irrational and inexplicable (for example, after reading Myers's *Scorpions*, debating whether the benefits of joining a gang are worth the risks). We also see how students gain greater understanding of each other and the cultures of others through these discussions. That is, we have seen the powerful role that literature can play in fostering tolerance, breaking down barriers, and building cross-cultural understanding.

We do not *teach* books. Instead, we *explore* books and their related themes with students. That is, we do not say to ourselves, "OK, *Journey to Topaz* [Uchida] is about the internment of Japanese Americans, so I'll use this book to teach students about this part of American history." However, we may select *Journey to Topaz* when the class is studying

World War II. We try to respect the literature and avoid turning reading and discussions into occasions for drilling students on factual information. While we hope that students will be better informed after reading such a book, we are also interested in following their lead. That is, we try not to impose our own agenda during the discussion. Instead, we listen carefully to the issues that students raise. But we do also raise issues that are important to us.

In some cases, issues that are important to us are less important to the students (for example, the stereotypical depiction of Native Americans in Lynn Reid Banks's *The Indian in the Cupboard* or of the mother in Oliver Butterworth's *The Enormous Egg,* where her only role was to cook for the men and keep their dirty boots out of the kitchen). In other cases, students raise issues that we had not considered (for example, that *The Cay* could be viewed as racist). This is the beauty of LSCs. The open-endedness of LSC groups allows for much more discussion of the students' interests than in traditional classrooms, where the teacher is in control of the questions and the discussion topics and direction.

In the remainder of this chapter we describe ways we believe LSCs can contribute to cross-cultural understanding.

Learning About Cultures from Books and Discussions

Reading books leads to increased knowledge about people living in different times and places. Just as Katharine was first introduced as a teenager to life in the United States through John Steinbeck's novels, so Gail's students are introduced to what it is to be a young black man through Walter Dean Myers's books. The facts of an event, an era, the life of a person, or a collective experience can be learned through a lecture, filmstrip, or textbook. LSCs allow us to go beyond these facts. The books and the discussions work together to draw us into the lives, times, and experiences of characters. It is one thing to know the facts of the internment of Japanese Americans during World War II; it is quite another to also feel the anguish of a family that has only hours to pack up its belongings for an indefinite and incomprehensible stay in a desolate, unknown location, as Yoshiko Uchida helps us experience in *Journey to Topaz.*

In Patricia Beatty's *Lupita Mañana,* a teenage sister and brother cross the border into the United States in search of an aunt. The story describes the harsh economic conditions that many experience in Mexico, which propel many to cross the border into the United States even though they do not have documents. The book describes the perils of crossing the border; the work of immigration officials; and the hopes, dreams, and sometimes inflated expectations of immigrants coming to the United States. After reading this book, Sylvia reflected on these realities and her own response in a literature log entry:

> I though that this book is really good and I think it must of been very difficult for Lupita and her brother to cross the border cause its a thing of death or life and they were risking their lifes and I also think that they are very brave but one thing I didn't really like was they did all that hard work and at the end they found out that their Aunty was not rich after all. I think that was messed up. Sorry of the language I just can't help it. I mean they risk their life's and look what they got. They got to work but poor Salvador he was send back to Mexico when the imigration caught them actually they only caught Salvador. Lupita was very lucky she escaped. Well I really liked the book.

Another favorite book among students is *Roll of Thunder, Hear My Cry* by Mildred Taylor. Through this book, we learn what life was like for poor, rural African Americans living in the south in the 1930s. This book captivates students and gives them insight into what it must have been like to grow up as a black child in a very hostile and prejudiced part of the country. Sylvia's written response to *Roll of Thunder, Hear My Cry* indicates that she identified with the black children and was incensed about how they were treated by the white people. In retelling sections of the book that particularly affected her, she demonstrates her awareness of the evils of prejudice:

> I think that this book is really a good example of being prejudice against Black people for example where littel man his sister and brother go to school and when the white kids pass by the black kids get splashed by the mud and the white kids don't get in trouble for that. I think that is awfully not fair. I am shure glad that they got their revenge by digging a hole so they could crash in it

and guess what they did? They had to walk all the way and specially the girls they were complaining alot about getting dirty with their fancy dresses and their shiny shoes. What I also though that was really mean was when those American kids gave the Black people those used beat up math books and in the back it showed how many times the white kids used them and they gave them to the black kids when they were all torn apart and the pages were missing and they were also very dirty. That was very awfull.

In many classrooms, students learn about prejudice and discrimination toward African Americans only when they study Martin Luther King, Jr., and the bus boycott. Such books as *Roll of Thunder, Hear My Cry, The Friendship, The Gold Cadillac,* and *Mississippi Bridge* (all by Mildred Taylor) introduce students to the experiences and history of African Americans living in the southern United States before World War II. After reading these books, many students comment that they had no idea what it was like to live in a segregated society. Several students who are not African American have also commented in discussions and in their literature logs that their parents hold a prejudiced view of African Americans, believing that they cannot be trusted and are thieves. Many of the students, particularly recent immigrants from Southeast Asia, know virtually nothing about African Americans, even though they often live in predominantly African American neighborhoods, where they are sometimes viewed as intruders. Older female relatives in Southeast Asian households may wear traditional clothing, which leads to taunts from neighborhood children and teenagers. Very few of the older Southeast Asians speak much English. This leads to misunderstanding and causes the American-born and immigrant groups to live separate lives that rarely intersect. In addition, many of the Southeast Asian immigrants have come from rural areas and small towns, a completely different experience from living in an American city. Given these facts, it should not be surprising that there is little cross-cultural interaction and understanding.

Mildred Taylor's books expose students to life in a segregated society. The books of African American writers such as Walter Dean Myers, Candy Dawson Boyd, and Joyce Hansen also engage them. In contrast with Taylor's books, these authors' books are set in more recent times and in urban contexts, which allows students to become more aware of the life experiences of their contemporaries. These books also provide affirmation for the African American students in the class, while enabling the others to view their African American peers and neighbors with more understanding and less hostility. It is hard to be prejudiced against a group of people whose lives one understands better.

Fahm read *Jump Ship to Freedom* (Collier and Collier), which takes place just after the Revolutionary War. The story is about the struggle for freedom of a young African American slave, Daniel Arabus. This book prompted Fahm to do some profound thinking on the relative merits of being alive but a slave, as opposed to being dead but free. She wrote about this in her literature log:

> I think that even though your not free from slavery and you have a chance to you should try and take that chance and even though you might get killed you and other slaves can know that you died trying and it's better than knowing that you died of hard work from slavery. I also think that you can't give up if you think your not going to make it. You should try and if you think you went for enough than your'e either going to make it or your'e either not but as I said it's better than dying of slavery and it's also better knowing that you died trying.

Many of the books that we have read for LSCs are grounded in unfamiliar cultures, at least for some students, and this has often led to rich discussions. Linda Crew's *Children of the River* introduces students to the war that led to the immigration of many Southeast Asians to the United States. The book describes customs that the students do not always understand or appreciate. During one discussion, Rosa shared a part of the book that she thought was funny—when the main character, Sundara, was taking a shower while wearing a towel. The group was confused over why she was wearing the towel, and the students were quick to make fun of it, as the following excerpt illustrates:

ROSA: You know, the part I really like. It was funny when she said, "We're not allowed to take our showers naked," in the, when she was in school.

ANGELINA: Oh, oh yeah.

ROSA: That embarrassed her, too, and I'm like, I wouldn't take showers over there.

(*Several students speak at the same time.*)

SYLVIA: That was weird about, when she's taking showers and the mom says that she can't see herself naked. She has to wear a towel.

ANGELINA: No, she can see herself naked, but other people can't.

SYLVIA: No, she said she can't see herself—

(*Several students speak at the same time.*)

ROSA: No, she can't see herself naked. When she was putting the shampoo on her head, she said, "I tried to open my eyes to see what was going on, but I couldn't because . . ."

GAIL: I think that I heard that in the Cambodian culture, too. Sometimes they wrap those long cloths—

SYLVIA: —towels, uh-huh—

GAIL: —around them as they shower.

SYLVIA: That's weird.

MARÍA: Why do they do that?

GAIL: That's a good question. I don't know.

MARÍA: They don't watch themselves when they take a shower?

ROSA: They do.

SYLVIA: They're all like, "Where's my foot?!"

It was clear that the students were confused about this custom. Gail didn't understand it either, so she talked about it with a Cambodian instructional assistant at lunchtime. She learned that in Cambodia most people do not have showers in their homes and use the river to bathe. In order to bathe in privacy, the women wrap themselves in long cloths that cover their bodies. Later in the day, Gail shared this information with the group of students, helping them understand a custom that had initially struck them as strange and funny.

Many of the students in Gail's class are immigrants from Southeast Asia who lived for some time in the refugee camps in Thailand. *Children of the River* evokes strong emotions among many of them. Choulaphone and Chansamone used the computer to correspond with each other about books. In one exchange, they discussed a dilemma that many immigrants face, whether to abide by their native customs or those of their new country. Chansamone wrote to Choulaphone, "I think Sundara should choose who she want to date or merry because she is in America now and she can disobeys her culture sometimes." In her response, Choulaphone agreed, "I think Sundara should do what ever she want to." This is an issue that many of the students face. Like Sundara, they often find themselves in conflict when the American way of life differs from the ways of their country of origin.

Many of the students felt so strongly about the value of reading *Children of the River* that they made specific recommendations about who they thought should read the book. Eata recommended the book for fellow immigrants. He wrote:

> A book that help my life was Children of the River. If you just came to America and know how to read, this book might help you think what it's like in coming to America when your from another country. Your life might not be the same as in Children of the River, but it will help you understand a little more about America and what it might be like when your from another country.

When Eata came to the discussion group, he raised this issue:

EATA: I would recommend it to people who just came from [to] America like for only two year. No, I mean like a sponsor. Then read it to see how they really feel.

GAIL: What did you mean when you said you'd recommend this book to sponsors?

EATA: Because some sponsor really wouldn't know how to feel.

GAIL: Um. So you thought this book really lets you see how somebody who just came to this country feels.

Sung considered both refugees and a wider audience when she wrote that she would recommend the book "to the people that would like to learn about how people escape from there country. And to people that had to leave there country because of the war."

Sometimes, books prompt students to share features of their own culture that others may not be familiar with. On one occasion, Samesi, a sixth grade Tongan student whose mother had recently died, read *Stone Fox* (Gardiner). In this story a boy's much-loved dog, Searchlight, dies heroically in a dogsled race. Through reading Samesi's literature log and listening to his comments in the LSC discussion, it was evident that this book had helped him come to terms with his own grief. It also prompted him to share an aspect of his own culture, one that was embedded in death and spirituality, as the following conversation excerpt illustrates.

RICHARD: I wonder if the dog really died.

MIGUEL: It says right here that his heart burst. Of course he's dead.

SAMESI: Even though he passed away, I think his spirit is still alive. Searchlight knew what Little Willie and Grandfather were going through. Little Willie had faith in himself. Searchlight knew what Little Willie and Grandfather needed. That's why they won the race. . . . It's disrespectful to say "dead" in our culture. That's not a good way. We say they passed away. When my mother passed, I heard her voice calling. My dad had a dream after my mother passed. She was on a plane and told him she had to go.

In just these few words, Samesi shared a great deal about his own culture, much of which was unfamiliar to the other students. It was clear that he trusted the group to treat his insights with respect and to understand and appreciate the importance of them, which they did. The group listened carefully, asked questions, and indicated to Samesi that they appreciated his sharing this information with them. Later, when the students were debriefing, Monica said, "I want to appreciate Samesi for sharing about his culture." Rhodora added, "Yeah, I appreciate Samesi, too, for talking about his mother's passing."

Sometimes students do not agree on the meaning of a custom or term, even if it is from their own culture, and through the discussion they negotiate meaning (even though they may not reach agreement). During a discussion on *Children of the River,* a group had been exploring what it was like to live in two cultures. The conversation began to focus on biracial marriages. Angelina mentioned a Mexican term, "pocha," which led to a vigorous exchange between three Latinas, Angelina, Sylvia, and Rosa, and a rather confused Filipino, Jarvis, as the following illustrates:

ANGELINA: When my brother, he had a pocha for a girlfriend and—
SYLVIA (*interrupting*): Oh, a Mexican American?
ANGELINA: He had a pocha, yeah.
JARVIS: A Porsche?
(*Several students say "pocha" very emphatically.*)
ANGELINA: And then he had—
GAIL (*interrupting*): Do you want to tell Jarvis what a pocha is?
SYLVIA: Pocha is, like, like, I'm a pocha because my parents are Mexican and I was born here.
ROSA: No, a pocha, a pocha.
(*Other students agree with Sylvia.*)
ANGELINA: Yeah, wanna bet?
ROSA: No, you know what a pocha is? A pocha is when your mom is, um, is Mexican, and your dad is American. That's a pocha.
ANGELINA: No.
SYLVIA: No, it ain't.
ROSA: Ask Daniel. Ask Daniel (*referring to another student in the class*).
ANGELINA: It says in the book, it says in the book, *Lupita Mañana*.
(*Students argue, disagreeing on this point.*)
ANGELINA: Read the book, read the book.
SYLVIA: Why do you think they're all, "Ah, there goes a pocha." Because her parents are Mexican and she was born *here*—
ANGELINA: Yeah, because (*inaudible*) in America.
ROSA: They're the same thing.
ANGELINA: Anyway.
SYLVIA: Anyway.

The Latina students brought prior experience to bear when discussing the meaning of the term "pocha." They were clearly familiar with its use, but could not agree on whether the term was grounded in differences in country of birth of two generations (parents born in Mexico and children born in the United States) or in differences in where their parents were born (mother and father not born in the same country). Later, Katharine checked with a friend who teaches Chicano studies. She explained that "pocha" or "pocho" are used to refer to Latinos who speak English, but cannot speak Spanish well.

Identifying and Examining Stereotypes

At times, the world can seem very confusing and contradictory, particularly when one is adjusting to a new culture. In LSCs, students frequently raise sensitive issues that the books have prompted. Sometimes they reveal very personal, and not very flattering, sides of themselves in their discussions and literature logs. One issue often talked about in LSCs is prejudice. For example, a group of students sat down one day to discuss Theodore Taylor's *The Cay*, a book set during World War II. The narrator is a Caucasian boy who was born in the segregated south of the United States, but is living in the Caribbean. He is befriended by an elderly black man, who dies while protecting the young boy. At the beginning of the discussion, the conversation focused on the front cover illustration and more literary features of the book. However, after about ten minutes, Laurie, an African American fifth grader, wriggled forward on the rug, thrust her head into the open space at the center of the circle, and spoke for the first time:

> I felt bad when I read this: "I saw a huge, very old Negro sitting on the raft near me. He was ugly. His nose was flat and his face was broad; his head was a mass of wiry gray hair. For a moment, I could not figure out where I was or who he was."

Laurie steered us to the page and added, "You don't hear, 'An ugly old whitey.' This book is very racist." The rest of the group was silent at first as they considered Laurie's comments, but then they began to concur with her, agreeing that the words seemed to be racist. But the discussion did not stop there. Laurie's comments acted as the catalyst for a long, often emotional, and very thoughtful discussion about the narrator's point of view and their own experiences with prejudice (their own prejudices and those of others).

On another occasion, during a second meeting on *Iggie's House* (Blume), the students were discussing the theme of the book. In this story, published in 1970, an African American family moves into a white neighborhood and encounters racism on the part of one of the neighbors, who refers to African Americans as "colored people." Rosa was the first to raise the issue of stereotyping when she said:

> I think, I think the theme was that everybody was the same. It doesn't matter how is your skin, it matters your heart. It doesn't matter if you are black or white because it really matters how you feel about the person that you really like or love.

Esmeralda expanded on Rosa's comment, indicating that she thought that one should judge a person on the kind of person they are, rather than on the color of their skin:

> I thought that this book was about telling what their feelings were inside and not with the color of skin 'cause if you like were racist, you'd say, "Ooh, I don't wanna hang out with them because they're black or colored." You know, you'd be racist. So, I thought, I think that the theme was to care about what their feelings are inside and not what their color of skin is outside.

María narrowed the discussion by asserting that she believed that the book was about race relations between African American and Caucasian people: "I think the book was about . . . African Americans and white people, and I think that they shouldn't care about the color of the skin, they should care who they are from inside." Tamara, the only African American in this discussion, pointed out that not all Caucasians are racists, and went on to explain that she thought the theme was how even though some people judge others based on the color of their skin, there are other people who don't. She said:

> OK. I think the theme of the book is like how people got treated about their colors and . . . how Winnie was really nice to them even though their color was different from hers. And I thought the book was basically about how she was really really nice to them, but how some people weren't nice to them, but she was really a good friend to them.

Sometimes when we talk about race and stereotypes, we tend to focus on differences between people. In a series of exchanges about *Iggie's House,* Angelina and Kim Lon point out similarities between people of all races. Angelina initiated the idea, pointing out how human beings share similar experiences:

> I think that the theme was that, they were telling you that everybody is the same, it's not just the color or the shape of them. Because they use the same peanut butter, and . . . she noticed that. So, she knows that everybody is the same . . . the difference is just their color.

Iggie's House has also led to discussions in which students have raised their own experiences with racism, as Guadalupe did:

> I think the book was about black people and white people. My brother's half white. I don't care if they're white. I'm Mexican, right? I'm not gonna tell my brother, "I'm not playing with you 'cause you're white!" So I don't think it's fair that the black people can't play with the white people, right?

Sean had also read *Iggie's House,* and during a discussion he commented that he had once held racist ideas about Asians:

> I think I might have been a little bit racist before coming to Hawthorne. I thought, "Oh, now I won't have any friends 'cause they're mostly Asians [there]." But after about two weeks we were like this (*holding up his index and middle fingers tightly together, indicating friendship*).

Sean went on to explain that he had come to realize that his earlier ideas were wrong and that he now had many good friends who were Asian.

The Blume book was also thought-provoking for Kae Hor, a Mien student, whose views about African Americans were different from those of his parents. He wrote about this in his literature log:

> The book made me feel sad because they wanted the black people to move because of there color. Like my parents just because people are black they are bad and mean people but they arean't. Some

are nice and kind but my parents they think they are bad people like the kind who robb houses and kill people. I have a black friend and my father says don't let him come in the house or he will steal your stuff. So that's why the book make me sad.

Many of the books that touched on racism led students to voice their own views on the subject. In some cases, they grounded their comments in day-to-day realities, offering pointed analogies, as Tamara did when commenting on how ridiculous it is for people to judge others based on skin color:

Everybody should like black because, like when you go to the store you see black jeans that people are always buying it . . . if they're white, they should only be buying like white clothes, and like not different colors like black or anything because it's color, they can only like white.

This discussion, which included Marci, a college student volunteer, went beyond comparing skin color to the color of clothes. Tamara noted the seriousness of this issue and how people have feelings, unlike a piece of cloth.

TAMARA: I think that's not fair.

KIM LON: Because it's color of the skin, and a color of the things.

MARCI: So why is it different?

TAMARA: Because it's like a person. They're talking about a person, and they're like, talking about material, so like it's really different because you can't say that a person would be a material and a material would be a person 'cause like, people have feelings, and like material really doesn't.

The discussion moved into the notion of stereotypes, and students openly shared stereotypes they had frequently heard about other ethnic groups:

ROSA: Some people think differently than us. I be hearing my friends, they were saying, "Oooh, African Americans don't take a shower, they'll always be stinky, they only take a shower once a week, or once a month."

MARÍA: And they say that's why they're black.

TAMARA: That's really a stereotype.

GAIL: What was a stereotype?

TAMARA: It's when you say, like, "Blondes are dumb." It's like an over-look of everybody else. It's when you think everybody else is the same thing because they're that color. . . . It's like when you say like, people that are Mien have lice, but that's not really true, because I know people that are Mien that really don't have it.

GAIL: That's a stereotype about Mien that you've heard before?

TAMARA: Yup.

MARCI: Where do you think stereotypes come from?

TAMARA: People that really don't know.

GAIL: Have any of you heard stereotypes about other people?

STUDENTS: Yeah.

GAIL: Like what?

ROSA: I be hearing people like African Americans, they always be stealing, breaking into houses, and getting stuff. That's why they don't like them. That's not right. That's never happened to me.

MARÍA: Some people say that when they see [an] African American doing something bad, they think that other African Americans are the same.

GAIL: They judge everybody because [of] maybe one person?

In the context of *Children of the River,* a group of students had been discussing marriage customs in Cambodia. What started as a lively critique of arranged marriages moved into a discussion of biracial marriages. Rosa talked about her mother's opposition to her marrying outside of her ethnic group. Rosa's willingness to share such a sensitive issue helped the whole group address it, while also supporting her:

ROSA: Like my mom telling that, "I don't want you to marry a Chinese boy." I'm like, "Why not?" 'Cause, like, this boy from my apartments, he likes me, he's Filipino. And then my mom's like, "I don't want you to marry a Filipino. Go out with Filipino." I'm like, "Why not? They're still people." And she's all like, "I don't want you. They stink." I'm like, "Mom, that doesn't really matter, you know." She's all like, "Well, anyways, I don't want you marrying with a (*inaudible*) or American." I'm like, "Mom, you're being racist." [My mom says] "I don't really care about it. I don't like Chinese people." But if I did marry a Chinese people, she's all like, "I'd kill you." I'll say, "Well, oh well."

SYLVIA: That's prejudice.

ROSA: I don't like when she's like that. I don't really like, maybe she—

SYLVIA (*breaking in*): Maybe she was mad or something.

MARÍA: You know—

ROSA: 'Cause she was mad at me—

MARÍA: 'Cause my mom—she's not like that. I'm like, "Mom, what if I marry some other people that's not like our culture?" I know, she's—

SYLVIA (*breaking in*): I know, she'd just say, "OK, that's your life."

MARÍA: I know she's like, "Well, if you really love him, you can marry him."

ROSA: My dad says you could marry whoever you want to because it's how you feel about them. Not if my mom likes them or not. That's when my mom was mad at me, though.

ANGELINA: Angry.

SYLVIA: 'Cause you must've done something, Rosa.

As these conversations illustrate, students were exploring how many stereotypes or misconceptions may come from a judgement about another culture, or from looking at another culture from one's own cultural biases. In one discussion, Tamara pointed out to the rest of the group that an action that may seem offensive to some cultures may be a natural practice in another culture. Tamara refers to an Afro-Carribbean religious practice, Santeria:

> But sometimes we see somebody, like an African American. They may have an animal, like a—I'm not sure, but they might be doing something to it, and then people might say that they're killing the animal, but maybe it's their religion to do that because they may not understand it. But people may think that they're doing something wrong.

This astute comment by Tamara added another dimension to the discussion of stereotypes. As she pointed out, people tend to look at the world through their own cultural lenses and are quick to judge others.

Increasing Understanding Through a Collaborative Learning Experience

In order to have in-depth discussions and truly learn from others, a safe, supportive environment must be created in the classroom, one in which no one is put down or judged for his or her ideas and opinions. Gail uses a program called *Tribes* (Gibbs 1994) where the ground rules of no put-downs, appreciation, mutual respect, attentive listening, and the right to pass help to establish a supportive classroom. A supportive and respectful classroom community is essential for exploring the important and some-times explosive issues that arise in LSCs. Teachers may work toward that goal in different ways; Gail has chosen to use the *Tribes* program to help foster a spirit of community.

In Gail's class, LSC groups are usually made up of students from a variety of backgrounds. The small group discussion format helps create bonds of respect and friendship. It will be harder for Gail's students to believe a stereotype about another ethnic group once they have talked with and listened to friends in LSCs and learned that they have much in common. Esmeralda and Rosa demonstrated this understanding when they evaluated their discussion about *Iggie's House:*

ESMERALDA: I thought this was a good discussion because some people are stereotype 'cause if they judge all African Americans by the thing that one person did.

ROSA: I think that this discussion was very good because we talk about everything. We talk about how people are not different, and there is—I think that everybody is different. Everybody is equal the same as we are.

Several of the books that the students have read touch on issues of racism and prejudice. It is particularly hard to raise personal issues that are grounded in one's own ethnic, religious, or cultural background. Usu-ally, students need to feel they can trust their classmates before revealing their thoughts and feelings, particularly when they have been the victims of racism. However, a safe and supportive classroom environment can foster this kind of sharing, which in turn can lead students to a deeper understanding of the impact of racism and to changes in how they treat other people. One day, Marie angrily recounted an incident that happened to her and another Laotian student:

MARIE: I remember when I was in third grade or second grade, the Mexican kid, when me and Ann were walking up the stairs, they called us "Chinese." They call every Asian "Chinese."

GAIL: So a lot of people believe that if you're Asian you're Chinese? (*Marie nods her head.*) They don't know the difference.

When students share personal experiences, as Marie did, they allow other students to learn from them. This type of cross-cultural learning was evident one day when a group was talking about *Children of the River*. Angelina began to refer to a Cambodian man as Chinese, but she corrected herself, as the following illustrates:

I thought that the story was never gonna end because, when the Chin—when the Cambodian guy died, I thought, "Who's she gonna like?"

Angelina has learned that there are different Asian groups. Marie's earlier reference to "Mexican" suggests the possibility that she does not realize that there are differences among Latinos. Although it is possible that the students to whom she was referring were all of Mexican descent, they may not have been, given the origins of the Latino population at the school.

One of our goals as teachers is to develop the kind of classroom environment where students feel that they can talk openly about incidents and attitudes that have been hurtful to them. In the process of doing so, we hope they will learn from their own experiences and be aware of how they treat other people.

At the fifth/sixth grade level, students frequently interact only with children of their own sex. They become very self-conscious around the opposite sex, and we often hear teasing about "boyfriends" and "girlfriends." The small group discussion format of LSCs brings boys and girls together to discuss books. Because there is a clear focus on content, students are more comfortable with each other than they appear to be at other times of the day. San Ching touched on this issue in an early evaluation of LSCs. At first, he writes, he was self-conscious around the girls in the group: "I think the circle is nervousing because I can't talk much around girls. I'm to shy. But I like it when there is more boys in the litera-ture circle." By the end of the year, however, he writes about how LSCs helped him feel more comfortable talking with girls: "When I first came to this class i couldn't talk in front of girls at all, but from the literature program I can talk in front of girls a little but still I am shy a little too."

In a diverse class, it is impossible for teachers and students to know the mores and values of all the different cultures. Inevitably, misunder-standings will arise, and even well-meaning and well-informed children and teachers may inadvertently offend others from a different culture. What is critical is that students and teachers feel free to raise their concerns with each other. LSCs contribute to the development of a trusting commu-nity of learners and can act as the catalyst for the discussion of issues that are often overlooked or ignored in many classrooms. Some teachers tell us that they are afraid to provide a forum for the discussion of potentially volatile issues; they fear that doing so will only exacerbate the problem. We have found quite the opposite to be true. We are constantly on the lookout for opportune and natural moments to encourage students to look more deeply at issues that address race, culture, gender, language, religion, special needs, social class, and political events and systems. Through open-ended discussions, we can all deepen our understanding of often controversial issues, while experiencing what it means to live in and develop a democratic world.

As Gail's students engaged in discussions about books grounded in cul-tures different from their own, they began to raise questions about why there were so few books about non–European American groups, includ-ing their own. In a discussion of *Children of the River* that involved five Laotian boys, the students commented on this:

SAN CHING: This is the only Asian book I've read.
NOPPHAVANH: Mines too.
CHANSAMONE: Mine too.
GAIL: Really? This is the first book about Asians that you've read?
CHANSAMONE: There's no book about Laos.

Eata pointed out that although they hadn't read any books about their own native culture, they had read some books about Asians, including

Journey Home (Uchida), *Jar of Dreams* (Uchida), *Journey to Topaz* (Uchida), *Sadako and the Thousand Paper Cranes* (Coerr), and *In the Year of the Boar and Jackie Robinson* (Lord). San Ching pointed out that *Children of the River* was the "first Cambodian book" that they had read. Although it was about a Cambodian, these young Laotian students identified very strongly with it. It was as if they were saying, "Here at last is a book that has people in it that look like us, and they have had experiences that our families have also had." Eata pointed out, however, that although they had read a book about Southeast Asians, still, "We've never read any book about Laos." This had a powerful impact on us, reminding us of how important it is to see ourselves in books, at least some of the time.

During this discussion, Angie Barra, a teacher in a family literacy program, was in the room and overheard the conversation. At the end of the discussion, she approached the group with an armful of books. Many of them were about Southeast Asia. She thought the students would appreciate them. The students were very excited.

ANGIE: This one's from Laos. But it's from the Hmong. But it *is* from Laos. It's really a neat story, if you guys want to borrow it.

SAN CHING: Is it in English?

ANGIE: It's in English. And this one is about Cambodians in the refugee camps. What happened to them.

(*Students ooh and aah and lean forward to look at the books.*)

NOPPHAVANH: Clay Marbles.

ANGIE: Yeh, they have clay marbles and it's called *The Clay Marbles*. It's about what happened to a little girl in a camp in Thailand.

NOPPHAVANH: It's long.

(*Angie offers to lend the books to the children.*)

EATA: I'm gonna read this.

CHANSAMONE: I wanna read this.

GAIL (*to Angie*): Look, you've got takers already. Look, they're dying to read it.

As this chapter has illustrated, it is critical that teachers provide learning experiences that build on students' experiences and cultures. It is also important to introduce students to new experiences and cultures. Many of the issues teachers find difficult to discuss—or even bring up—in class emerge naturally in the course of discussing books. Through interacting with each other and teachers, students can negotiate meaning and search for answers to the hard questions we all must confront in today's world. LSCs are a valuable tool for addressing and clarifying these important issues. We know adults who meet in special groups to discuss issues similar to those that the eleven-, twelve-, and thirteen-year-old students in Gail's class are dealing with in LSCs.

Students have many explanations for the injustices they see around them. They have strong opinions, and sometimes their opinions differ from those of their parents. LSCs provide a setting where their opinions are valued, which fosters students learning about each other. As a consequence, they begin to break down stereotypes they may have. They learn to work side by side and engage in respectful and challenging discussions with peers and adults who speak different languages and represent different racial and ethnic groups. They continually celebrate diversity, not at one specific time of the year or on a special holiday, but every day.

Chapter 5

What Next?

Writing this book has been a tremendous learning opportunity. It has allowed us to reflect on our pedagogies and, more specifically, our current thinking on LSCs. We have looked carefully at how students have responded to learning events that reflect what we believe about reading theory and practice. This process of reflection has enabled us to recognize both the strengths and limitations of LSCs as they exist for us right now. Although, like other teachers, we continually make adjustments in the classroom, writing together has caused us to step back and examine even more carefully why we do what we do and what we would like to do differently in the future. We see this concluding chapter as a beginning, an opportunity for us to explore issues relating to LSCs that we feel are of particular importance.

The Role of the Teacher in LSCs

Even after they have been introduced to other approaches, many teachers teach in the same way they were taught. In the United States, this means that classrooms tend to be teacher-centered. Successful LSCs involve a much more student-centered approach, and this can be difficult for teachers to adapt to.

Gail began her career as a teacher who relied heavily on textbooks and accepted the idea of the teacher as all-knowing. When she became concerned about students being bored and hating to read, she gave them choices of what to read, but still expected students to answer questions for which she was seeking a particular answer. Later, when Gail was introduced to LSCs, she began to realize that reading is a transactional process and the role of the teacher should be one of facilitator rather than source of knowledge and judge. This view of teaching coincided with Gail's growing concern that students who did not have opportunities to think and work cooperatively in school would be at a disadvantage in an increasingly complex and technologically sophisticated society. Gail's classroom is now much more learner-centered and democratic than it ever was in the past. However, while writing this book, she looked critically at her teaching practices and identified several areas that she would like to work on (such as becoming more of a co-participant in discussions and learning to be more reflective).

Students can also have a hard time adjusting to a student-centered classroom. As we lead LSC discussions, we sometimes notice that students are directing their comments to us rather than to the entire group. This is particularly true for students who are new to LSCs, or at the beginning of each year, when students are becoming acquainted with each other. We remind students that the purpose of the discussion is to have a dialogue that involves everyone. Nevertheless, this idea is clearly new to many students, so we have learned to rely on certain strategies to encourage students to talk with each other. One of the most effective mechanisms we have found is to take written notes of the discussions, particularly at their beginning—and to keep our heads lowered as we do so. This is not always easy, because we like to give full attention to people who are speaking, but it can be a very effective way to encourage students to talk with each other, rather than to us. Also, the notes we take are helpful when it comes time to review the content of the discussion with the students. We have also found that the content of books and the emotional responses they generate greatly affect the amount of student-to-student interaction.

When students engage in regular, open-ended discussions, they eventually realize that the point is not to prove that they have read the book or to respond to known-answer questions generated by the teacher. So, while we continue to be uncomfortable when students direct their comments to us, we have learned to be patient.

Other issues of interactions with students have not been so easy to solve. In reading our transcripts of LSCs, we have noticed one issue in particular: our tendency to dominate discussions.

Over the years, we have prided ourselves on not dominating LSC discussions, but our transcripts reflect occasions when our comments have taken up, say, half a page, while the students' utterances take up only one or two lines each. This tends to happen when we are discussing books or issues that particularly interest us. Of course, quantifying length and number of utterances is not, by itself, an adequate assessment of how effective we are. We know that it is important for us to share our own experiences and response to the books. However, we also know that, if we are to foster student-centered conversations, it is important that we not dominate the discussions. We have found that audio- or videotaping or having another person keep detailed notes of discussions are simple, but powerful, ways to provide us with data we can use to reflect on our role as LSC teachers.

Including More Books by Authors from Underrepresented Groups

We have seen how enthusiastically students respond to books written by authors from their own cultures or books that are grounded in experiences with which they are familiar. For example, when a group read *The Star Fisher* (Yep), in which the main character is a young girl who has to translate for her mother, several students referred to similar experiences they had had. They talked about difficult or embarrassing situations that they had encountered as the translator for family members. Esmeralda mentioned how her mother was once returning a toaster and was very angry with the clerk because it wouldn't work. She wanted Esmeralda to translate word for word what she said. Esmeralda told the LSC group, "I was so embarrassed. I didn't tell the man what my mother said. I just said, 'the toaster doesn't work.' " Whenever a book touches on students' lives, they immediately become animated. Gail's students come from culturally and linguistically diverse backgrounds, and they rarely see themselves or their cultures in books. Despite growing interest in multicultural children's and young adult literature, only a small percentage of books are written by authors from underrepresented groups.

Many students have voiced their disappointment in not being able to read books that are grounded in their home cultures and life experiences. This is particularly so in the case of Southeast Asian and Latino children, as so few books have been written by or about these groups. In Chapter 4 we cited the positive reactions of a group of Laotian boys to Linda Crew's *Children of the River*. We were struck by their excitement at seeing their part of the world and their life experiences represented in the pages of a book. We believe it is very important for children to see themselves in books, as well as learn about other people in books.

Although Gail's LSC books now include several titles by authors from underrepresented groups (such as Walter Dean Myers, Mildred Taylor, Yoshiko Uchida, and Laurence Yep), she would like to expand her collection, particularly with books by and about Latinos and Southeast Asians. When selecting books, we seek out good writers who are either members of underrepresented groups or who have been scrupulous about accurately and sensitively portraying a culture to which they do not belong. Regardless of whether or not teachers are working in multilingual and/or multicultural classrooms, we think that all children benefit from reading about a wide range of experiences. We hope that the list of authors and illustrators from underrepresented groups provided in Appendix B will be a useful resource to other teachers.

Balancing the Needs of Both Fluent and Less Fluent Readers

It is important to establish a deadline for the completion of LSC books so that students can pace themselves and be prepared for discussions. Even though we solicit input from students when deciding on deadlines, problems can still arise. For example, as LSC groups often include both fluent and less fluent readers, it is not unusual for an experienced reader to take a book home and finish it before the next school day, whereas other students will need a week to ten days to finish it. If deadlines take into account the needs of the less fluent readers, the more fluent readers may have difficulty remembering the details of a book completed several days earlier. Conversely, if discussions are scheduled to take into account the needs of the more fluent readers, then some less fluent readers may not have enough time to finish the book. Thus, good scheduling is often a delicate balancing act. Generally, we schedule our first meeting so that all students will have finished the book; this often involves their reading both in school and at home. Even so, some students feel rushed. When Malcolm, a conscientious, careful reader who seemed to need more time to prepare for discussions than was usually available, reflected on LSCs at the end of the year, he wrote the following:

> Ms. Whang gives us too little time. I want to really get into the book. I don't like the way you should finish on a certain day. If you take your time in reading the book, the more you'll like it.

It is important also to offer LSC books of different lengths and levels of complexity so that students can select books that do not overwhelm them. This is particularly important for students who are new to LSCs, for struggling readers, and for students who are acquiring English as a nonnative language. Books in the student's native language would also help. Sometimes struggling readers select books that seem to be much too challenging for them; in these cases we try not to talk them into reading shorter, less complex books. We have learned to resist this temptation. Our overriding goal is to encourage students to become informed and independent readers; so while we frequently make recommendations about books to students, we leave the final decision of which book to read up to them. Their decisions frequently reflect the fact that reading is a social act: decisions are often made collaboratively, by two or more students, who then support each other as they read the book.

We believe that one characteristic of a fluent reader is the ability to select books independently. Although LSCs offer students choices, the ultimate decision-making is up to the teacher, who selects the books. Feedback from students about the books offered for LSCs indicates that they enjoy the selections and appreciate being exposed to authors and books that they may not have encountered otherwise. However, we are concerned that students who rarely read books outside of LSCs do not get much experience in making informed reading choices on their own. Perhaps LSCs should be alternated with independent reading sessions that are accompanied by small group discussions. In this way, less fluent readers would have opportunities to become familiar with more books, make choices over what they read, and still have the chance to explore books with other readers. Another idea we have been experimenting with is alternating LSCs with pair reading (two students select a book that they read and discuss together). Perhaps the best solution would utilize LSCs, pair reading, and independent reading with small group discussion. Whichever approach is used, however, it is essential to give students the chance to talk about the books once they have finished reading them. We have found that there is both a human and an intellectual need for readers to come together and share experiences in this way.

Post-Reading Activities

In many classrooms, the reading of literature is frequently accompanied by a plethora of book-related activities—book reports, posters, dioramas, writing assignments. Since seeing firsthand the power of LSCs on students' attitudes to books and hearing them comment on how much they get out of the discussions, we have abandoned most of the traditional post-reading activities, such as book reports or writing another chapter, preferring instead to allow more time for reading, written reflection, and discussion. Although we do not regret the decision to eliminate the inauthentic post-reading activities, we wonder if we are limiting the possibilities for response, particularly in the case of students whose preferred or strongest mode of response is not verbal. We have therefore begun to invite students to consider additional ways of exploring and responding to books. We suspect that for this to be successful we will need to make a concerted effort to introduce students to ways in which people respond to literature in the world outside of school: how choreographers and composers are inspired by a piece of literature or art; how professional book reviewers inform and influence readers (which makes their work very different from school book reports); how writers are often inspired to experiment by the work of another writer.

Even when students are encouraged (as opposed to obliged) to respond in other ways and are given choice over such things as the content and form of their response, and whether to do so independently or as part of a group, problems of interpretation of the task can occur. Katharine remembers the first time that she invited an LSC group in one of her college classes to continue responding to the book. Some students said that they would like to read more by the author, Mildred Taylor. This struck Katharine as an authentic follow-up activity. Another student said that she would like to write a different ending for the book. Although Katharine wondered why the student would want to do that rather than write her own story, she said nothing, concerned that any query might undermine the student. It wasn't until recently that Katharine discovered that the student had felt obliged to continue responding somehow—and came up with an activity that she had been required to do in elementary school. What was particularly startling was that the student believed that Katharine had told her what to do! Since then, we ask students to explain or clarify their choices—and allow them to decline further activity, if they wish.

Cross-Age LSCs

For several years, Gail and a first/second grade teacher, Mary Pippitt, have successfully implemented a cross-age reading program (Samway, Whang, and Pippitt 1995). One day, because the fifth and sixth graders were having such positive experiences with both LSCs and the buddy reading program, we talked about the possibility of integrating the two. We didn't do a great deal of planning or preparation; we just jumped right in. Gail asked the students if any were interested in leading a buddy-reading LSC. Twelve students volunteered. We thought it would be difficult for one older student to lead a group of four or five younger children, so we decided to have teams work with the younger students. We began experimenting. The students who wanted to lead an LSC stayed in Gail's class, and the remaining students went over to Mary Pippitt's class, where they continued with the usual buddy-reading program. This first experience was quite successful. In the debriefing session, it was clear that the students were very excited and proud of their accomplishments, and wanted to continue. At the same time, they remarked on how difficult it was when students didn't speak up or weren't paying attention.

We began to offer the students some preparation. They read several picture books and had small LSC group discussions with Gail. Although the older buddies initially selected the books they would read with or to their buddies, after a while the younger children made the selection. The older students prepared for booktalks by writing brief synopses of the books they had read. At the beginning of a buddy-reading LSC both the younger and older students would gather on the rug for booktalks and the selection of books. Then, for the next twenty minutes or so, groups of four younger children and two older children would meet to read and discuss the books.

Some of the older students, such as Fahm, demonstrated impressive skills as a teacher. She was patient and calm, even when something surprised her. She handled disruptions unobtrusively, by removing distracting objects or placing her hand on a younger child's hand to indicate that he or she needed to pay attention. She would paraphrase what group members had said and express appreciation for their comments. However, many of the cross-age conversations tended to be rather formulaic and static. It was as if the older students had come to the discussions with a set of questions they were anxious to run through (What did you like about the book? What did you think about the book? Did this remind you of anything that happened to you?). These types of questions are the kind that have often led to rich discussions among the fifth/sixth graders. What was different was that the older students were firing the questions at the younger children, often ignoring what a child had just said. It seemed as if they were uncomfortable with silence, something that adult teachers also experience when they are new to LSCs. We also noticed that sessions that began with open-ended questions often moved into yes-no questions, which further limited the range of the discussion. In the following example of this type of staccato conversation, Darron and Nopphavanh are leading the discussion:

DARRON: How about you, Mary, what do you like about the book? Would you like to read what you wrote in your literature log?
NOPPHAVANH: What you like about the book? Do you think it was good?
DARRON: Do you think it's sort of like any other book?
LILY: Me?
DARRON: Anybody.
ROBERT: OK, yeah.
DARRON: What book?

ROBERT: Huh?

DARRON: What book do you think it's the same to? Like sorta alike?

NOPPHAVANH: Do you think this book is the same compared to the other books you guys have read?

DARRON: Do they have a lot of rhymes like this?

ROBERT: No.

DARRON: Have you ever read any book that has a lot of rhymes like in *Bring the Rain to Kapiti Plain?*

LESLIE: Yeah.

DARRON: What book? The same, like, rhymes.

ROBERT: *The Dinosaur* or something.

DARRON: What was your favorite part about the book? How about you, Leslie, what do you think was your favorite part?

LESLIE: I don't know, it's funny.

When assessing the buddy-reading LSCs, two common reactions emerged: the older students enjoyed the experience, but they sometimes found it difficult to be a leader. In commenting on how much she enjoyed leading a buddy-reading LSC, Fahm wrote, "I think that the little kids learn how to speak up more and they learn what being a student in the literature meetings feel like." She also remarked how the older students had learned "how to get the meeting back into place if it gets of the track and they also learn how to do a book talk." We spent quite a bit of time in debriefing sessions dealing with difficulties that the leaders had encountered. They came to realize that being a leader—a teacher—was often very difficult. Fahm commented in her log, "The older kids learn that mostly what we go through is what almost all the teachers go to [through] they have to be patience with the kids when they don't speak and thats how the older kids feel when the little childrens don't speak up." She also remarked on how difficult it is when group members don't talk: "Sometimes it's not fun when their not talking but I learn that you got to give them time to do it they don't have to just come right out and say it you got to encourage them to talk and say what they thought about it."

The buddy-reading LSCs foundered after a few weeks, despite the entreaties of some of the students. Although we sensed that some of the problems would have worked themselves out had we stuck with it, we realized that, in order to have a successful buddy-reading LSC, much more planning, preparation, and training were needed. Because of the press of other activities, we put the idea on hold. But we would like to return to it in the future. We've been encouraged by the suggestions that students have made. Travera pointed out the importance of having "books that the kids really like" so that "they would talk more." Manop recognized the importance of planning and preparation; he wrote, "Another way that the buddie reading program could improve is that we should plan ahead before we meet. I could write down question on a paper too and think of what I should say during the meeting." Manop is correct: in order to implement a successful buddy-reading LSC program, both teachers and students need to be well prepared. Though we are satisfied with the way in which we spontaneously introduced buddy-reading LSCs, and we think the idea has a lot of promise, when we return to it we will do it in a more thoughtful way.

Reflecting About Writing

At the end of each LSC discussion, we ask students to comment on the session, an idea we have borrowed from the *Tribes* program (Gibbs 1994). Students usually comment on the degree to which the conversation was interesting and stimulating. Sometimes they comment on the contributions (or lack thereof) of individual group members and explore ways in which the meeting could have been more dynamic. They also comment on what they learned. We teachers contribute to these assessments of the group process.

Because we believe that discussions about books can help us all as writers, we have begun to ask students to comment on what they have learned about writing from reading and talking about a book. This has not been an easy thing for students to do, at least initially, perhaps because it is not something they are used to doing. However, it is a natural extension to the process of asking group members to revisit a book, when we often explore literary elements. Students may notice how an author creates dialogue and incorporate this into their own writing. Or they may comment on how it was hard for them to get into a book at the beginning because an author used too much descriptive language. We have not yet explored the influence of LSCs on students' writing, but this is something that we would like to do. Getting students to reflect on what they have learned about writing from reading books is one way to examine LSCs and writing.

Teaching Reading Strategies and Literary Elements

In this book we have made several brief references to teaching students about literary elements and reading strategies. When students in an LSC group talk about how people in the book change and seem so real, we may bring up the idea of character development. When they talk about how evil a particular character is, we may bring up antagonists and protagonists. When students comment on how long it took them to read a book, we may teach them reading strategies that can speed up their reading, such as not subvocalizing or pointing to the text while they read. All these have been spontaneous "teachable moments," which are very valuable—but they are sporadic. Although follow-up sessions often rely on student's being familiar with literary issues such as theme, plot, and narrative voice, we wonder if we have spent enough time helping them really understand these concepts and terms, many of which are new for them. Being immersed in books can help struggling readers gain confidence and fluency. We have noticed, however, that they often continue to struggle. While it is critical that students have choice over what they read and plenty of time in class to read and talk about books, we are shortchanging students if we do not also teach reading strategies.

A great deal could be accomplished if we were to devote about ten minutes each day to a whole class minilesson on literary elements. In order to meet the reading strategy needs of individual students, we could confer regularly with individuals and small groups. We must ensure that struggling readers have access to reading strategies that successful readers use. For example, when struggling readers tell us they do not know the meaning of a word and we ask them what they do to figure out the meaning, they invariably refer to only one strategy: "sound it out" (phonics). This strategy alone has not worked for them and continues not to work for them, so we must teach them additional strategies to add to their repertoire—for example, making an informed guess based on context and then using phonics to confirm or disprove their prediction.

Once we began to ask students to comment on what they had learned about writing from the books they had read in LSCs, we discovered that simply asking this question is a very effective strategy for helping them make connections between what published writers do and what they could do as writers. We believe that it would be even more helpful to focus more on teaching reading strategies and literary elements, also.

Varying the LSC Selections

We tend to follow a routine when offering LSC selections. Usually the books are novels, often written by different authors. We have experimented with themed selections (for example, books about immigration to the United States) and books written by a particular author (for example, Mildred Taylor), but we think it would be helpful to vary the selections more. In particular, we would like to incorporate nonfiction, poetry, and picture books.

Many students prefer reading and writing nonfiction, and we believe that including this genre in LSCs would allow students to appreciate the content and writing of nonfiction even more. Katharine has begun to include nonfiction books for LSCs in her college classes. So far, she has found that discussions tend to focus heavily on content. This is not surprising, given the nature of nonfiction books. However, the groups do also draw on personal experiences and discuss literary devices that nonfiction authors use when writing and/or illustrating.

Poetry is another genre that many students enjoy, but so far we have not had much experience integrating it into LSCs. Several options are available: bringing in multiple copies of the same book of poetry, offering different books of poetry by the same author, selecting books of poetry by different authors that share a common characteristic or theme, and using poetry anthologies that include many authors, styles, and themes. Katharine has introduced poetry in her LSCs with teachers. Perhaps because the collections that she has included have focused on free-form rather than rhyming poems, discussions have tended to focus on definitions of poetry and such literary devices as line breaks and punctuation.

As for picture books, Gail has used them only rarely in LSCs, except in buddy-reading LSCs. Usually, she has brought in picture books only when there have been several students who are very new to English. Like many upper grade teachers, she rarely uses picture books with older students. However, becoming more familiar with this genre has made her aware of the richness of its stories and illustrations, which all students could benefit from experiencing. In addition, exploring picture books in depth with peers and adults helps the older students as they prepare to work with younger students in buddy-reading (Samway, Whang, and Pippitt 1995).

Assessment

We are often asked whether LSCs have improved students' reading proficiency. Gail is obliged by district policy to administer a norm-referenced, standardized reading test at the end of each year. After the first year with LSCs, her students' scores on the comprehension part of the test were significantly higher than those of the children in classes that were not doing LSCs. However, we are both leery of using such test scores to evaluate the impact of LSCs on students' reading achievement because these tests do not assess reading in a contextualized, authentic way. We do believe that the amount of reading and exploring of books that students engaged in enhanced their reading comprehension, a critical component in reading that Gail's students had had a great deal of difficulty with in the past.

Just visiting a classroom when LSCs are in session provides compelling evidence of their value. Some students are enthusiastically talking about books, which they have chosen and actually read. Other students are immersed in their reading. Still others are writing about books in their literature logs. This contrasts with the many classrooms we have been in where students are bored and disenchanted with reading activities that are designed to teach them how to read, but do not teach them the thrill of reading.

Of course we need to be able to assess each individual student's reading strengths, progress, and needs. To that end, we have collected many boxes' worth of data (for example, literature logs, lists of books read, reading surveys, transcripts of LSCs, student evaluations of LSCs, and field notes) that attest to the development of the students as readers and thinkers. Gail keeps notes on LSC group members (see Figure 8 in Chapter 2), and although her form is effective in guiding her when she summarizes a discussion and in monitoring student preparation for and participation in discussions, it has limitations from an assessment point of view: several students are listed on a single page, and it is tedious to cut up the pages into slips of paper for filing away in individual students' folders. Gail found that she tended to file away the uncut sheets and not refer to them when assessing individual students. Katharine has found peel-off address labels inserted into students' folders to be a more manageable and useful way to record students' comments, behavior, and reading strategies.

In the future, we would like to place more emphasis on a systematic, authentic assessment of students' reading development. We would like to collect data several times during the year (for example, reading surveys and reading records two to three times a year) so that we can make informed instructional decisions geared to the needs and interests of students. These data would also be useful for student self-assessment. We would like to confer more regularly with students about their reading processes, strategies, skills, and struggles, and be more assiduous about recording and following up on the content and outcome of these conferences. These records would provide us and the students with valuable information when assessing their growth as readers. Experience tells us that simply providing struggling readers with opportunities to select and discuss books is not usually enough to turn them into fluent, confident, effective readers. It helps a great deal, but we also need to assess the performance of less fluent readers, in particular, so that we may teach them appropriate skills and strategies to enable them to succeed in secondary school and beyond.

Continuing to Develop Our Own Literacy

There are days when we wonder if we have done the best job possible when leading LSCs. For example, after a session we may wonder if we missed an opportunity to help students understand a literary device that could have enhanced their understanding of a book or be a useful resource to them as writers. It is on days such as these that we are most aware of the fact that we do not often engage in book discussions with knowledgeable peers, and we vow to remedy the situation. Because we enjoy talking about books with others and would like to continue to develop our own literacy, we would like to be members of adult LSC groups that read and discuss children's, young adult, and adult literature. We have already begun to make plans to take part in such a group.

When we read professional books, we sometimes get the impression that the authors have "cracked the code"—found answers to all their questions. However, now that we have written this book, we find we have more questions than we can probably handle in the immediate future. Some of these questions (for example, the need to include more books by authors from underrepresented groups) occurred to us before we wrote the book. However, others (for example, how to balance our wish to fully contribute to discussions without overwhelming students) arose out of our writing. Although the range of issues that we would like to explore more fully in the future may occasionally seem overwhelming, we are stimulated by the opportunity to put our most current thinking about LSCs into practice.

Appendix A

Books That Have Been Enjoyed by Students in Fifth/Sixth Grade LSCs

Armstrong, William H. (1969) 1972. *Sounder*. New York: HarperCollins.

Atwater, Richard, and Florence Atwater. (1938) 1978. *Mr. Poppers Penguins*. Illus. Robert Lawson. New York: Dell.

Babbitt, Natalie. (1975) 1985. *Tuck Everlasting*. New York: Sunburst Books.

———. (1977) 1989. *The Eyes of the Amaryllis*. New York: Sunburst Books.

Banks, Lynne Reid. 1982. *The Indian in the Cupboard*. New York: Avon.

Beatty, Patricia. 1992. *Lupita Mañana*. New York: Morrow.

Blume, Judy. (1972) 1976. *Otherwise Known as Sheila the Great*. New York: Dell.

———. (1972) 1976. *Tales of a Fourth Grade Nothing*. New York: Dell.

———. (1974) 1978. *Blubber*. New York: Dell.

———. (1971) 1978. *Freckle Juice*. New York: Dell.

———. 1981. *Superfudge*. New York: Dell.

———. (1970) 1986. *Iggie's House*. New York: Dell.

Boyd, Candy Dawson. 1984. *Circle of Gold*. New York: Scholastic.

———. 1986. *Forever Friends*. New York: Puffin.

———. 1988. *Charlie Pippin*. New York: Puffin.

Burnett, Frances Hodgson. (1905) 1975. *A Little Princess*. New York: Dell.

———. 1986. *Sara Crewe*. New York: Scholastic.

Butterworth, Oliver. (1956) 1987. *The Enormous Egg*. Illus. Louis Darling. New York: Dell.

Byars, Betsy. (1980) 1983. *The Night Swimmers*. Illus. Troy Howell. New York: Dell.

Carlson, Natalie S. (1958) 1989. *The Family Under the Bridge*. Illus. Garth Williams. New York: HarperCollins.

Chetin, Helen. 1982. *Angel Island Prisoner*. Trans. Catherine Harvey. Illus. Jan Lee. Berkeley, CA: New Seed.

Chew, Ruth. 1976. *Trouble with Magic*. New York: Dodd, Mead.

Cleary, Beverly. (1970) 1981. *Runaway Ralph*. New York: Dell.

———. 1982. *Ramona Quimby Age 8*. New York: Dell.

———. (1975) 1984. *Ramona the Brave*. New York: Dell.

———. (1951) 1990. *Ellen Tebbits*. New York: Avon.

———. (1953) 1990. *Otis Spofford*. New York: Avon.

———. (1973) 1990. *Socks*. New York: Avon.

———. (1968) 1992. *Ramona the Pest*. New York: Avon.

Coerr, Eleanor. (1977) 1994. *Sadako and the Thousand Paper Cranes*. New York: Dell.

Cohen, Barbara. 1990. *Molly's Pilgrim*. Illus. Michael J. Deraney. New York: Bantam.

Collier, James Lincoln, and Christopher Collier. 1983. *War Comes to Willy Freeman*. New York: Dell.

———. (1981) 1987. *Jump Ship to Freedom*. New York: Dell.

Conrad, Pam. 1991. *Stonewords: A Ghost Story*. New York: HarperCollins.

Courlander, Harold. 1987. *The Cow-Tail Switch and Other West African Stories*. New York: H. Holt.

Crew, Linda. (1989) 1991. *Children of the River*. New York: Dell.

Dahl, Roald. (1978) 1988. *Fantastic Mr. Fox*. New York: Puffin.

———. (1982) 1989. *The BFG*. New York: Puffin.

———. (1988) 1990. *Matilda*. New York: Puffin.

Danziger, Paula. (1980) 1988. *The Cat Ate My Gymsuit*. New York: Dell.

———. (1980) 1988. *There's a Bat in Bunk Five*. New York: Dell.

Davidson, Margaret. 1991. *I Have a Dream: The Story of Martin Luther King*. New York: Scholastic.

Dorris, Michael. (1992) 1994. *Morning Girl*. New York: Hyperion.

Estes, Eleanor. (1944) 1974. *The Hundred Dresses*. Illus. Louis Slobodkin. New York: Harcourt Brace.

Fleischman, Sid. 1987. *The Whipping Boy*. Illus. Peter Sis. Mahwah, NJ: Troll.

Fox, Paula. (1985) 1988. *Maurice's Room*. Illus. Ingrid Fetz. New York: Macmillan.

———. (1973) 1991. *The Slave Dancer*. New York: Dell.

———. (1991) 1993. *Monkey Island*. New York: Dell.

Gardiner, John R. (1980) 1983. *Stone Fox*. Illus. Marcia Sewall. New York: HarperCollins.

Gates, Doris. (1940) 1976. *Blue Willow*. Illus. Paul Lantz. New York: Puffin.

George, Jean Craighead. 1974. *Julie of the Wolves*. Illus. John Schoenherr. New York: HarperCollins.

———. (1988) 1991. *My Side of the Mountain*. New York: Puffin.

Greenfield, Eloise. (1974) 1987. *Sister*. Illus. Moneta Barnett. New York: HarperCollins.

Hansen, Joyce. 1986. *Yellow Bird and Me*. New York: Clarion Books.

———. (1980) 1989. *The Gift-Giver*. New York: Clarion Books.

———. (1988) 1992. *Out from This Place*. New York: Avon.

Ho, Minfong. 1993. *Clay Marbles*. New York: Farrar Straus & Giroux.

Howe, Deborah, and James Howe. 1980. *Bunnicula: A Rabbit Tale of Mystery*. Illus. Alan Daniel. New York: Avon.

Howe, James. 1983. *The Celery Stalks at Midnight*. Illus. Leslie Morrill. New York: Macmillan.

———. 1983b. *Howliday Inn*. Illus. Lynn Munsinger. New York: Avon.

Keene, Carolyn. 1980. *Secret in the Old Lace*. New York: Simon and Schuster.

Lord, Bette Bao. 1986. *In the Year of the Boar and Jackie Robinson*. Illus. Marc Simont. New York: HarperCollins.

MacLachlan, Patricia. (1985) 1987. *Sarah, Plain and Tall*. New York: HarperCollins.

———. (1988) 1990. *The Facts and Fictions of Minna Pratt*. New York: HarperCollins.

Mathis, Sharon Bell. 1986. *Sidewalk Story*. New York: Puffin.

———. (1975) 1986. *The Hundred-Penny Box*. Illus. Leo and Diane Dillon. New York: Puffin.

Mazer, Anne, ed. 1993. *America Street: A Multicultural Anthology of Stories*. New York: Persea.

Meltzer, Milton. 1988. *Mary McLeod Bethune*. New York: Puffin.

Miles, Betty. (1976) 1989. *All It Takes Is Practice*. New York: Knopf.

Moore, Emily. 1991. *Just My Luck*. New York: Puffin.

———. 1991. *Something to Count On*. New York: Puffin.

Myers, Walter Dean. (1988) 1990. *Scorpions*. New York: HarperCollins.

Naidco, Beverley. (1986) 1988. *Journey to Jo'burg: A South African Story*. Illus. Eric Velasquez. New York: HarperCollins.

Naylor, Phyllis R. 1992. *Shiloh*. New York: Dell.

O'Dell, Scott. (1970) 1976. *Sing Down the Moon*. New York: Dell.

————. 1989. *Black Star, Bright Dawn.* New York: Fawcett.

————. 1990. *My Name Is Not Angelica.* New York: Dell.

Park, Barbara. (1982) 1983. *Operation Dump the Chump.* New York: Avon.

————. 1988. *The Kid in the Red Jacket.* New York: Knopf.

————. (1982) 1989. *Skinny Bones.* New York: Knopf.

Paterson, Katherine. (1977) 1987. *Bridge to Terabithia.* Illus. Donna Diamond. New York: HarperCollins.

————. (1978) 1987. *The Great Gilly Hopkins.* New York: HarperCollins.

Pitts, Paul. 1988. *Racing the Sun.* New York: Avon.

Shyer, Marlene Fanta. (1978) 1988. *Welcome Home, Jellybean.* New York: Macmillan.

Sleator, William. 1979. *Into the Dream.* New York: Dutton.

Smith, Doris Buchanan. (1981) 1990. *Last Was Lloyd.* New York: Puffin.

————. (1973) 1992. *A Taste of Blackberries.* Illus. Mike Wimmer. New York: HarperCollins.

Smith, Robert Kimmel. 1984. *The War with Grandpa.* Illus. Richard Lauter. New York: Dell.

————. (1978) 1994. *Chocolate Fever.* New York: Dell.

Soto, Gary. 1991. *Baseball in April and Other Stories.* New York: Harcourt Brace.

Spinelli, Jerry. (1990) 1992. *Maniac Magee.* New York: HarperCollins.

Staples, Suzanne F. 1989. *Shabanu: Daughter of the Wind.* New York: Knopf.

Steig, William. (1976) 1984. *The Real Thief.* Illus. by author. Farrar, Straus & Giroux.

Sterling, Dorothy. 1987. *Freedom Train: The Story of Harriet Tubman.* New York: Scholastic.

Taylor, Mildred. (1975) 1984. *Song of the Trees.* New York: Bantam.

————. (1987) 1989. *The Friendship.* New York: Bantam.

————. (1987) 1989. *The Gold Cadillac.* New York: Bantam.

————. (1976) 1991. *Roll of Thunder, Hear My Cry.* New York: Puffin.

————. (1987) 1992. *Mississippi Bridge.* Illus. Max Ginsberg. New York: Bantam.

Taylor, Theodore. 1977. *The Cay.* New York: Avon.

————. (1989) 1993. *The Trouble with Tuck.* New York: Avon.

Uchida, Yoshiko. 1985. *Journey to Topaz.* Illus. Donald Carrick. Berkeley, CA: Creative Arts.

————. (1978) 1992. *Journey Home.* Illus. Charles Robinson. New York: Macmillan.

————. (1983) 1993. *The Best Bad Thing.* New York: Macmillan.

————. (1981) 1993. *Jar of Dreams*. Illus. Leslie Ward. New York: Macmillan.

Vuong, Lynette Dyer. 1992. *The Brocaded Slipper and Other Vietnamese Tales*. Illus. Mai Vo-Dinh. New York: HarperCollins.

Wagner, Jane. 1972. *JT*. Photos by Gordon Parks. New York: Dell.

White, E. B. (1970) 1972. *The Trumpet of the Swan*. Illus. Edward Frascino. New York: HarperCollins.

————. (1952) 1990. *Charlotte's Web*. New York: HarperCollins.

Yarbrough, Camille. 1989. *The Shimmershine Queens*. New York: Bullseye Books.

Yep, Laurence. (1975) 1977. *Dragonwings*. New York: HarperCollins.

————. (1977) 1990. *Child of the Owl*. New York: HarperCollins.

————. (1989) 1992. *The Rainbow People*. New York: HarperCollins.

————. 1992. *The Star Fisher*. New York: Puffin.

Appendix B

Authors and Illustrators of Literature for Children and Young Adults Who Are Members of Underrepresented Groups

An asterisk indicates that the person has written and/or illustrated picture books. He or she may also have written longer texts.

AFRICAN AMERICAN/AFRICAN CARIBBEAN

Angelou, Maya*
Bambara, Toni Cade
Battle-Lavert, Gwendolyn*
Berger, Terry
Berry, James
Bontemps, Arna
Boyd, Candy Dawson
Brooks, Gwendolyn*
Bryan, Ashley*
Bundles, A'Lelia
Burroughs, Margaret
Butler, Octavia
Byard, Carole*
Caines, Jeannette*
Charles, Oz
Childress, Alice
Clifton, Lucille*

Collier, Eugenia
Cooper, Floyd*
Crews, Donald*
Cummings, Pat*
Deveaux, Alexis
Dillon, Leo*
Douglass, Frederick
Ellis, Veronica Freeman*
Evans, Mari
Feelings, Muriel*
Feelings, Tom*
Fields, Julia
Flournoy, Valerie*
Gilchrist, Jan Spevey*
Giovanni, Nikki*
Graham, Lorenz
Graham, Shirley

Greene, Bette
Greenfield, Eloise*
Grimes, Niki
Guy, Rosa
Haley, Alex
Hamilton, Virginia
Hamlin, Willie T.
Hansen, Joyce
Haskins, Francine*
Haskins, James
Havill, Juanita*
Holbert, Raymond*
Howard, Elizabeth Fitzgerald*
Hudson, Wade
Hughes, Langston
Humphrey, Margo
Hunter, Kristen
Jackson, Jesse
Jonas, Ann
Jones, Angela
Lawrence, Jacob*
Lester, Julius
Marshall, Paule
Mathis, Sharon Bell*
McKissick, Frederick*
McKissick, Patricia*
Mendez, Phil*

Moore, Emily
Morninghouse, Sundaira
Musgrove, Margaret*
Myers, Walter Dean
Patrick, Denise
Patterson, Lillie
Pinkney, Andrea
Pinkney, Brian
Pinkney, Jerry
Price, Leontyne*
Ransome, James*
Reynolds, Barbara
Ringold, Faith*
Robinson, Adjai*
Steptoe, John*
Strickland, Claudia
Tate, Eleanora*
Taylor, Mildred
Thomas, Ianthe
Thomas, Joyce Carol
Walker, Alice*
Walter, Mildred Pitts
Wilkinson, Brenda
Williams-Garcia, Rita
Wilson, Johnniece Marshall
Yarborough, Camille*

CAMBODIAN/CAMBODIAN AMERICAN

Chiemroum, Sothea*
Lee, Huy Voun*
Wall, Lina Mao*

CHICANO/MEXICAN/LATINO

Acuna, Rudy
Ada, Alma Flor*

Anaya, Rudolfo*
Ancona, George

Anzaldúa, Gloria*
Argueta, Manlio*
Brusca, María Cristina*
Cedeño, Maria E.
Cisneros, Sandra
Cruz, Manuel
De Garza, Patricia
Díaz, Jorge*
Felipe, Juan*
Flores, Barbara*
Flores, Enrique*
García, María*
García, Richard*
Garza, Carmen Lomas*
Gomez, Cruz*
Griego, Margaret

Hermanes, Ralph
Hernández, Irene Beltrán
Jimenez, Francisco
López de Mariscal, Blanca*
Maestro, Jorge
Martinez, Ed*
Méndez, Consuelo
Mendoza, George
Mora, Pat*
Orozco, José Luis*
Rosairo, Idalia
Sánchez, Enrique O.
Sandoval, Ruben
Soto, Gary*
Zubizarreta, Rosalma*

CHINESE/CHINESE AMERICAN

Ai-Ling, Louie
Chan, Harvey
Chan, Jennifer*
Chang, Monica
Chin, Charlie*
Chin, Frank
Chin-Lee, Cynthia*
Chong Lau, Allen
Hong, Lily Toy*
Hou-Tien, Cheng*
Huang, Chen Zhi
Lee, Gus
Lee, Wendy*
Liu, Saho Wei

Lord, Betty Bao
Louie, Ai-Ling*
McCunn Lum, Ruthanne
Sing, Rachel*
Tan, Amy*
Wang, Rosalind
Wong, Jade Snow
Wong, Shawn
Wu, Di
Yee, Paul
Yen, Clara*
Yep, Laurence*
Young, Ed*

FILIPINO/FILIPINO AMERICAN

Aruego, Ariane*
Aruego, Jose*
Villanueva, Marie*

JAPANESE/JAPANESE AMERICAN/JAPANESE CANADIAN

Akaba, Suekichi*
Aliki*
Anno, Mitsumasa*
Hamanaka, Sheila*
Hayashi, Akiko*
Hidaka, Masako*
Ichikawa, Satomi*
Igus, Toyomi
Ikeda, Daisaku
Iko, Momoko
Isami, Ikuyo*
Iwamura, Kazuo*
Iwasaki, Chihiro*
Kanome, Kayoko*
Kasja, Tejma*
Kawaguchi, Sanae*
Kikuchi, Isao*
Kimura, Yasuko*
Kishida, Eriko
Kitamura, Satoshi*
Kobayashi, Yugi*
Kobeyashi, Robert*
Koide, Tan*
Komaiko, Leah*
Maruki, Toshi
Matsuno, Masaka*
Matsutani, Miyoko
Miyazawa, Kenji

Mizumura, Kazue*
Mori, Toshio
Morimoto, Junko*
Murayama, Milton
Nakatani, Chiyoke*
Namachi, Saburo*
Otani, June
Sakai, Kimiko*
Sakuri, Rhoda*
Say, Allen*
Shikegawa, Marlene*
Soya, Kiyosha*
Takashima, Shizuye*
Takeshita, Fumiko*
Tejima, Keraburo
Tomioka, Chiyoko
Tsuchida, Yoshiharu
Tsuchiya, Yukio*
Tsutsui, Yoriko
Uchida, Yoshiko*
Watanabe, Chigo*
Watkins, Jeanne Wakatsuki
Watkins, Yoko
Yagawa, Sumiko*
Yamaguchi, Tohr*
Yashima, Taro*
Yoshi*

KOREAN/KOREAN AMERICAN

Choi, Sook Nyul
Kim, Young Sook
Lee, Marie G.
Paek, Min*

LAOTIAN/LAOTIAN AMERICAN

Xiong, Blia*

NATIVE AMERICAN/CANADIAN

Ata, Te*
Black Elk
Blue Eagle, Agee
Bluenose, Philip
Brown, Dee
Bruchac, Joseph*
Campbell, Maria
Deloria, Vine
Dorris, Michael
Ekoomiak, Normee*
Harper, Maddie*
Highwater, Jamake
Hungry Wolf, Beverly
King, Edna
Kusugak, Michael Arvaarluk*
Littlechild, George*
Manintonquat
Momaday, Scott
Ortiz, Simon*
Parker, Arthur
Regguinti, Gordon*
Sanderson, Esther*
Sandoz, Mari
Sneve, Virginia Driving Hawk*
Sterling, Shirley
Tapahonso, Luci
Taylor, Drew Hayden
Thompson, Sheila*
Wallis, Velma
Walters, Anna Lee
White Deer of Autumn*
Yamane, Linda*

PUERTO RICAN

Algeria, Ricardo
Colorado, Antonio
Delacre, Lulu*
Lasanta, Miriam
Martel, Cruz
Mendez, Consuelo*
Mohr, Nicholasa

THAI/THAI AMERICAN

Ho, Minfong
Vathanaprida, Supaporn

VIETNAMESE/VIETNAMESE AMERICAN

Huynh, Quang Nhuong
Lee, Jeanne M.*
Mai, Vo-Dinh*
Quyen, Van Duong
Tran, Kim-Lan*
Tran-Khan-Tyuet*

References

Bird, L. B., and L. P. Alvarez. 1987. "Beyond Comprehension: The Power of Literature Study for Language Minority Students." *Elementary ESOL Education News* 10 (1): 1–3.

Daniels, H. 1994. *Literature Circles: Voice and Choice in the Student-Centered Classroom.* York, Maine: Stenhouse Publishers.

Edelsky, C. 1988. "Living in the Author's World: Analyzing the Author's Craft." *The California Reader* 21: 14–17.

Eeds, M., and R. Peterson. 1991. "Teacher as Curator: Learning to Talk About Literature." *The Reading Teacher* 45 (2): 118–26.

Eeds, M., and D. Wells. 1989. "Grand Conversations: An Exploration of Meaning Construction in Literature Study Groups." *Research in the Teaching of English* 23 (1): 4–29.

Gibbs, J. 1994. *Tribes: A New Way of Learning Together.* Santa Rosa, CA: Center Source Publications.

Peterson, R., and M. Eeds. 1990. *Grand Conversations: Literature Groups in Action.* New York: Scholastic.

Rosenblatt, L. M. 1978. *The Reader, the Text, the Poem: The Transactional Theory of the Literary Work.* Carbondale, IL: Southern Illinois University Press.

———. (1938) 1983. *Literature as Exploration.* 4th ed. New York: Modern Language Association.

———. 1991. "Literature—S.O.S." *Language Arts* 68: 444–48.

Samway, K. Davies, G. Whang, C. Cade, M. Gamil, M. A. Lubandina, and K. Phommachanh. 1991. "Reading the Skeleton, the Heart, and the Brain of a Book: Students' Perspectives on Literature Study Circles." *The Reading Teacher* 45 (3): 196–205.

Samway, K. Davies, G. Whang, and M. Pippitt. 1995. *Buddy Reading: Cross-Age Tutoring in a Multicultural School.* Portsmouth, NH: Heinemann.

Short, K. G., and K. M. Pierce, eds. 1990. *Talking About Books: Creating Literate Communities.* Portsmouth, NH: Heinemann.

Smith, K. 1990. "Entertaining a Text: A Reciprocal Process." In *Talking About Books: Creating Literate Communities,* edited by K. G. Short and K. M. Pierce. Portsmouth, NH: Heinemann.

Weaver, C. 1994. *Reading Process and Practice: From Socio-Psycholinguistics to Whole Language.* 2d ed. Portsmouth, NH: Heinemann.